THE CUCKOOS' NEST

500 Years of Cambridge Spies

Christopher Catherwood

OLEANDER

The Oleander Press
16 Orchard Street
Cambridge
CB1 1JT

www.oleanderpress.com

ISBN: 9781999900458

A CIP catalogue record for the book is available from the British Library.

The KGB called five of their Cambridge spies The Magnificent Five. My wife has five wonderful great-nephews, the grandsons of her brother the late Sterling Moore and his wife Janet. So this book is therefore dedicated to a very different "Magnificent Five", my five great-nephews: Tyler and Garrett Crabbe, Sam, Tate and Jack Moore and to their truly magnificent great-aunt, my wife Paulette.

CONTENTS

FOREWORD

As Christopher Catherwood points out, spy stories – the real ones, that is – seem to have an endless fascination for us. When these stories have a connection with an ancient university and a charming city, then the fascination is all the greater. In this extraordinarily readable book, Catherwood explores the connection between place and intrigue, between a university committed to truth and people committed to dissemblance. The result is an extraordinarily rich narrative.

Of course there has been a great deal of ink spilled over the various spies who populate this book. There are numerous studies of the central figures in the group known as the Cambridge spies – Philby and his colleagues have been the subject of almost every sort of scrutiny, and have the distinction of appearing in film, drama and fiction rather more than most historical characters of their period. One might have thought that fresh perspectives on what they did would be hard to create, and yet this book has achieved that – and in a very engaging way – by putting them in the context of Cambridge, and by drawing surprising historical parallels between twentieth century spies and their antecedents from the same university. The activities of the Cambridge spies of the modern age, it seems, have roots in the world of espionage of Marlowe and Walsingham – suspicion and secrecy, of course, are nothing new.

Yet even if Christopher Catherwood stresses this continuity of espionage, he has interesting things to say on spies of our own time – the post-Cold War era. He asks how the Russian Federation recruits its foreign spies today, and suggests that the modern state would have a difficult time of it in finding ideologically-motivated agents prepared to betray their own country. That is a particularly interesting thought, as it certainly appears to be the case that a number of the spies who have come to light in recent years have been purchased rather than recruited because they believe in a cause. And yet there is the interesting phenomenon of the modern "whistle-blower" spy who reveals what his own country has been up not by passing secrets to an opposing state, but by making them public. This sort of spy might be considered the equivalent of those spies who were motivated by loyalty to communism as an ideology. In each case there is the notion of there being a greater loyalty that trumps loyalty to one's own country.

Of course the psychology and motivation of the individual spy will always depend on a combination of influences and factors. Christopher Catherwood dwells on the significance of the Cambridge setting, but he is also sensitive to the many other experiences and influences that made people like Anthony Blunt and Kim Philby what they were. Blunt is perhaps the most interesting of all these cases, and the author's treatment in this book provides us with a particularly succinct and plausible account of a much-discussed life. Blunt, in a way, is like the university that produced him: elegant, nuanced, discreet, intellectually distinguished and refined. He could not have been the product of an earnest redbrick institution: Cambridge was the perfect setting for him. He is, of course, an easy target: a man brought up in privilege, leading the life of an aloof and aristocratic scholar – a man to whom the rules did not apply. All of that is clear enough, but he was much more than that, and much of his mystery, it seems, remains. At the end of the day, though, what he did was appalling, particularly when we remember, as Ben Macintyre points out in *Double Cross*, that by passing information to German-infiltrated Soviet intelligence, Blunt could so easily have compromised the Allied landings in Normandy. And that sort of consideration gives a particular edge to this fascinating study of a city and its spies: the world of Cambridge, calm and civilized, was right next door to a world that was anything but that.

Alexander McCall Smith

PREFACE

Although this is distributed by a University Press in the United Kingdom, it is what historians call a work based upon secondary sources, especially since it is about espionage, and most of the primary sources are, by their very nature, not available, or certainly not able to be seen for an extra length of time beyond the normal thirty years closure.

I have, therefore, been able to use a wide variety of secondary literature, especially the many fascinating works by Cambridge historian Professor Christopher Andrew, who is not only the Official Historian of MI5 but someone who has, in effect, invented a whole new line of historical enquiry: Intelligence History. Christopher was writing books on the secret world long before the tap on the shoulder came from MI5, and I am among those who have benefited enormously by his opening up of new sources for historians and for interested members of the general public.

And since, for all but the very few, Christopher's books are the *only* source, his contribution in delving through the archives has been especially helpful. But as always, the interpretation that you are about to read is entirely mine and, while I am one of those privileged enough to attend his always gripping seminar on Fridays in Cambridge, he has not been part of the writing of this book, and there may well be areas in which we disagree or have come to different conclusions.

I mention this as endless references to "as Christopher Andrew says" or "as Oleg Gordievsky and Christopher Andrew conclude" would be boring, and as this is a book for a wider audience, there are also no footnotes.

I have usually referred to the books that I have read on the first appearance, and I have been fortunate that Cambridge University has an enormous number of volumes on espionage from the sixteenth century through to the twentieth. Many of these books were written before the official history by Christopher Andrew, and some are by Russian authors who have a fascinating angle of their own.

However, before this book I have never seen any work that takes Cambridge spies all the way from the sixteenth century, from Walsingham and Marlowe, down to the infamous Cambridge traitors of the 1930s (of whom my book also shows that there were more than the Magnificent Five). And I think that my synthesis is wholly new as well, albeit inspired by the great British novelist Graham Greene, who realised decades ago the close similarities between the Catholic spies of the sixteenth and friends of his like Kim Philby in the twentieth.

AN INTRODUCTION

Cambridge, a city in the middle of the flat and often watery fenlands in the eastern part of England, is famous not as a market town, which it has been for centuries, but for its university, now just over 800 years old. If we are going to look at the 'Cambridge spies' we ought briefly to understand something about Cambridge and the way in which it works.

Sometimes it is one half of the term 'Oxbridge', meaning England's two medieval founded universities, of which the first, Oxford, in the heart of England, is the older of the two, and indeed so ancient that it has no official starting date. Cambridge, the junior, began life when some academics, unhappy with life in Oxford, left for the remote eastern wastes of the country, somewhere around 1209, and founded a university where a bridge crosses the river Cam: Cambridge.

However, Cambridge is more than just a university. It is also a federation of colleges, all of which proudly guard their statutes and their status. Since the nineteenth century and the rise of large-scale science, the university has been able to develop faculties and laboratories not related to the colleges but to the central body itself. The most famous of these being, for example, the Laboratory of Molecular Biology (LMB), funded through the British government's Medical Research Council since 1947 (and before then it was part of the university's famous Cavendish Laboratory). But the LMB is on the outskirts of Cambridge in a hospital complex, and although its staff have won 13 Nobel Prizes for work done in the laboratory (plus a further eight to people visiting the facilities), most Cambridge students today would have no idea where it was.

Similar things could be said for the high technology Centre for Mathematical Sciences, hidden behind trees in a site in the west of Cambridge – some of the world's best mathematic minds reside there but the average undergraduate outside that discipline would not even know it exists.

Today, with so many Cambridge students being postgraduates, based primarily in their faculties or in libraries, and from all over the world, the intimate Cambridge of earlier years is something that they might have read about but not experienced – in at least one college reserved for graduates, the authorities had to invent 'high table' and a dinner with gowns because the students complained at missing out on authentic Cambridge traditions! (At graduate level professors and pupils usually eat and chat together informally at meals and coffee breaks – a far cry from the ancient traditions of the university!)

But for most *undergraduates* Cambridge has, in one sense, not changed since the middle ages, and for students in the humanities subjects, where most teaching is done within college, even less. (Science pupils have to spend time in laboratories, which are university based.)

And socially it is very much the same since the days of Christopher Marlowe at Corpus Christi College, or Kim Philby at Trinity College; college friendships, across academic disciplines, are the norm, and college sports clubs, dining halls and drinking at the college's own bar are as vital a part of everyday life as they have been for centuries. (The names of Cambridge colleges often reflect a religious origin – Trinity after the Christian Holy Trinity and Corpus Christi is the Latin for the body of Christ.)

This is because while a student is accepted to study, say, History or Biology at the University of Cambridge, the only way to enter the university is to be accepted by an individual college, through which you will be taught, and, if the college is wealthy enough, in which you will live for your three to four years as an undergraduate. Colleges are all interdisciplinary, with medical students living next door to those studying Latin, and in the bar a chemist might find herself sitting next to a historian while ordering a pint.

Cambridge does have intercollegiate societies, the most famous of which is the Cambridge Union Society, a debating club mainly used for a cheap meal in central Cambridge but long a training ground for would-be politicians and TV presenters, many of whom have held elected office in the society. The biggest is unexpected – the Cambridge Inter-Collegiate Christian Union (or CICCU) is over a century old and has countless vicars and missionaries from among its former members. And there are political, sporting and lifestyle clubs of all shades and varieties, some ephemeral and others, like the actors of the Footlights, still producing some of the most famous comedians and actors of our time.

Colleges have their own clubs, of the same variety, and for our book one has particular eminence – a society for debating, mainly comprised of King's and Trinity college members, popularly known as the Apostles. Much conspiratorial nonsense has been written about the Apostles, which began in the nineteenth century among the more radically-inclined and still exists today, having officially secret but, in reality, probably rather boring and anodyne discussions on a range of intellectual topics. However, during the 1930s many of its members were Marxist, some were gay, and, notoriously, some were both...

While many colleges have postgraduates, who are more faculty-based and often from another country, normally undergraduates get to know each other in the way that students at that same college have for centuries. And, as such, it is usually with your college that your primary loyalty lies. Most colleges went co-ed in the 1970s and 1980s, while three of the colleges originally founded for women still remain exclusively female.

Colleges vary in size – Trinity, where many of the subjects of this book were educated, is enormous, whereas some of the others, such as Trinity Hall, are much smaller and happy to stay that way.

Similarly, there is a vast discrepancy in wealth – as we shall see in the Philby chapter. Trinity is fabulously rich, helping to subsidise much of the rest of the university through the Isaac Newton Trust, whereas others are much poorer, with tiny endowments, and in one recent case, New Hall became Murray Edwards College out of gratitude to a prosperous donor in whose honour it was renamed.

The oldest Cambridge college is Peterhouse, founded in 1284, and one of the best-known modern colleges is Churchill, founded in honour of Sir Winston Churchill in 1960, and famous for its links with science. Trinity was founded by King Henry VIII in 1546 (on the proceeds of merging several medieval institutions which he had abolished), and King's is also a royal foundation, by the unfortunate King Henry VI in 1441. But the college of two of our spies, Trinity Hall, was founded in 1350 by a Bishop, and the Guild of Corpus Christi founded their eponymous college two years later in 1352. One of the wealthiest colleges in the university, and geographically one of the largest (alongside Trinity and Churchill) is St John's, founded by Lady Margaret Beaufort in 1511, and which, so unique to a place like Cambridge, brags about its six Nobel Prize winners, six former prime ministers – and two saints!

Two of the colleges founded for women that have remained single-sex (Newnham and Girton), were founded in the nineteenth century, and Cambridge also has colleges for mature students next to each other (St Edmund's College, which is mixed and with over sixty nationalities, and Lucy Cavendish, which is for women only). And in the 1960s many colleges were founded exclusively for postgraduates, such as Wolfson or Clare Hall.

So a Cambridge experience will be very different, say, from a student who 'reads' Latin at an old college like Trinity Hall, and one who studies Engineering at a recent college like Churchill. Looking at medieval buildings might be fun for visitors, but coping with plumbing that is hundreds of years old is a very different matter...

Such is the unique world of Cambridge and its colleges. Spies are still being educated here, thankfully now for our own side rather than that of our enemies. Sir Richard Dearlove, who was educated at Queens' College and is now Master of Pembroke College, served as Director of the Secret Intelligence Service (MI6) during the Iraq war. Hugh Bicheno was, like John Harvard, the great Puritan and founder of the university named after him in the USA, educated at Emmanuel College, joined MI6 and has written about his adventures in his thrilling book *Razor's Edge*. But today entrants to the secret world have to take the same exams as anyone wanting to join the civil service, and the days of a tap on the shoulder from a discreet don to have a glass of sherry with a chap in Whitehall are long gone.

PART I

We start the story with two people actively involved in espionage from the sixteenth century, the Elizabethan era, when England was under threat from Spain and came close to being invaded in 1588. As you will see, there were several Cambridge-educated spies, especially in the dark tale of Christopher Marlowe.

A CLIMATE FOR TREASON
CHRISTOPHER MARLOWE

The book that, in 1979, exposed the 'Fourth Man', Sir Anthony Blunt, keeper of Queen Elizabeth II's pictures, as a Soviet spy, was called *The Climate of Treason*.

But Cambridge in the sixteenth century, in the reign of Queen Elizabeth I (1558–1603) was very much a hotbed of treason, intrigue, double-dealing and spying for foreign powers for ideological reasons. As was the same university in the 1930s, when Philby, Blunt and others decided to spy for the Soviet Union and betray their own country.

When we come to look at the twentieth-century spy Kim Philby, we can remember an analogy used by his fellow MI6 agent, the writer and novelist Graham Greene. In speaking of Philby, Greene, a devout convert to Roman Catholicism, likened the spies of his own era, who supported Marxism and the USSR, to the Catholic missionaries to England in Marlowe's century, who risked their lives for their faith and who supported Rome over England. If we can see sixteenth-century spies in that modern, secular, twentieth-century light, the issues they faced and the battles they fought become more accessible to us.

Students the world over love causes, whether protesting against the Vietnam war in the 1960s or in favour of saving the planet in our own times. 1580s Cambridge and its 1930s equivalent were no different. What had changed were the cause, and the names.

In 1585, when Marlowe's portrait was painted, England had an external enemy: the Spain of King Philip II. Three years later, in 1588, the Spanish would launch a great invasion fleet – the Armada – to try to conquer the country, depose Queen Elizabeth I, and re-impose Roman Catholicism as the official English religion as it had been under her sister Queen Mary, cousin and briefly, wife, of Philip II himself. We now know that the rosy official version of England's history under the 'Virgin Queen' (Virginia was named for her) was in many parts myth. While much of the nation had genuinely converted to the Protestant version of Christianity which she espoused, and which her father King Henry VIII had introduced in the 1530s in order to divorce Mary's mother and marry hers (Ann Boleyn), thousands of others remained loyal to the Roman Catholic faith to which most English people had belonged for centuries.

Today we no longer associate a version of Christianity with patriotism, but in England, certainly up to the nineteenth century, being English (or after 1603, being British) and Protestant went very much hand in glove. To be Catholic was to be on the same side as our national enemies, whether Philip II and Spain in the sixteenth century or King

Louis XIV and France in the late seventeenth and early eighteenth centuries. Even now, as British readers will know, the official state church is still called the Church *of England*, even though actual church attendance outside Christmas or Easter is increasingly small, and as the country is now multicultural, with many of the remaining professing Christians either Catholic or some kind of non-state church Protestant.

So to be Catholic in the 1580s was not just a religious statement but a political one as well, and one that smelled, to the Elizabethan authorities, not just of heresy but of treason.

And 1930s Cambridge was not much different, if one substitutes Stalin and the USSR for Philip II and Spain, and Marxist-Leninist communism for Roman Catholicism. To be a communist was to be a supporter of the Soviet Union, the overthrow of the capitalist system upon which Britain was based, and to follow a regime which, to many in the 1930s, was far more threatening than what we now know to be the even more lethal and dangerous Nazi menace of Germany and fascist threat of Italy and Franco's version of Spain. To be a Catholic was to support the great power that threatened England's very existence every bit as much as the existential menace of Soviet tyranny during the cold war.

Or to put it another way, the personal was profoundly political.

This was the Cambridge to which a young Christopher Marlowe came in the 1580s, to Corpus Christi College. Then, as now, first degree students lived and were taught in colleges – teaching through the university itself came later

– and membership of a college was, and remains, the prime source of loyalty and community for undergraduates, from the Middle Ages right through to the present.

Corpus (as in *Corpus Christi*, Latin for the 'Body of Christ') was founded in 1352, in this case a rare instance of an Oxford or Cambridge college not having a rich founder patron (such as Lady Margaret Beaufort for St John's College in Cambridge, or King Henry VI for King's College) but a guild, such as often existed in medieval times, that of Corpus Christi. The college has always been one of the smallest in Cambridge – Trinity College, where the 1930s spies Philby, Burgess and Blunt were educated, for example, is huge, fabulously rich (it owns the O2 arena in London, the former Millennium Dome, and the land of Felixstowe docks) and has over 30 Nobel Prize winners. Corpus was never that rich, and has a different atmosphere. Indeed, perhaps because of its poverty, much of the Corpus that Marlowe would have known is still there – the Old Court, built in the fourteenth century, remains essentially unchanged to this day, and was not demolished for new housing in the way that many colleges at both Oxford and Cambridge were vandalised by over-enthusiastic Victorian rebuilders in the nineteenth century. Watch a play in Old Court, as countless Cambridge students and visiting American and Japanese tourists do today, and you are doing so in exactly the same spot in which Christopher Marlowe would have done as an undergraduate back in the 1580s.

As well as ideology, there is also the element of danger in having strong beliefs that can get you into serious trouble or even cost you your life. In my own student days, I spent time behind the pre-1989 iron curtain, with Hungarian or Czech dissident friends oppressed by the Soviet Union. It was exciting and thrilling – and enormous fun – but the ever-present element of danger gave it an extra frisson, that made it both scary and heroic at the same time.

It was the same for young Catholics in England in the 1580s, and Marxists in the 1930s; a belief that was all consuming, and which, precisely because there was considerable danger attached, made it all the more daring and attractive. It is often joked that the best way to sell a book or a DVD is to ban it, and the illegality of Catholicism and later of treasonable Marxism gave a strong cachet to those who believed it.

It is perhaps not surprising that homosexuality – illegal both in the 1580s and in the 1930s – also bonded people together and that it is possible that Marlowe was gay, as were some of the Cambridge spies, such as Guy Burgess and Anthony Blunt, centuries later. Being underground in one area of one's life made it equally attractive to be subversive in others, such as ideology or the cloak and dagger world of espionage. But we are not entirely sure which way Marlowe swung, and Philby, for example, was completely heterosexual, so we can exaggerate the effect of sexuality on the Cambridge spy networks of Elizabethan and modern times.

Let us look first at what made Marlowe famous, then at his spying career, and finally at his murder, which remains as mysterious in the twenty-first century as it was back in 1593.

Marlowe was baptised in Canterbury, the great cathedral city of England, on February 26 1564. He was the second but oldest surviving child of John Marlowe, a skilled shoemaker (who long outlived his wayward son) and his wife Katherine. It was, therefore, a similar skilled craftsman background to that of his contemporary William Shakespeare, now the more famous playwright of the two. Elizabethan society was in many ways a golden age, as we shall see in more depth in the chapter on Sir Francis Walsingham, Elizabeth's great spymaster, but it was also profoundly violent, with death often around the corner, and without the degree of law enforcement that we take for granted today. Marlowe father and son were involved in what were then called affrays, some being vicious assaults and, in one case, an act of sexual violence when young Marlowe was but a teenager. His temper, like that of his longer-living father, was to become notorious, and the fact that he was to die a bloodthirsty death is thus perhaps no coincidence.

Then, in 1578, he won a scholarship to King's School, Canterbury, one of the oldest church-founded secondary schools in the world, which opened in 597, and one of whose recent pupils was Michael Morpurgo, the author of *War Horse*.

But in those days pupils went to university earlier than they do today, and in 1580 he won a prestigious Parker Scholarship to Corpus Christi College at Cambridge, where his portrait still exists, discovered near his old rooms. (While some scholars doubt the painting's authenticity, most, including many now at Corpus, regard it as genuine, including an eminent member of MI5 at Corpus today.) At Cambridge just before him was Richard Poley, at Clare College, and someone who was to crop up regularly in

Marlowe's life, including at his mysterious end and murder in 1593. Of Poley's espionage career we know a great deal, as he was one of the most important spies in the Elizabethan period, including, as we shall see, playing a pivotal role in the Babington plot to overthrow and murder Queen Elizabeth – without his intelligence the conspiracy could perhaps have succeeded, and with disastrous consequences...

As will become apparent in the Walsingham chapter, Elizabethan England was what we would now call a police state. There was an elected parliament, and some political dissent was tolerated, albeit grudgingly. But the atmosphere, even in a university town like Cambridge, could probably be quite scary – and indeed one could argue *especially* frightening since Cambridge, then as now, was at the heart of heated intellectual and moral/religious debate, and the wrong views on many of those subjects could prove literally fatal, with burning at the stake and death on the torture rack being just two of the outcomes for having the wrong kind of views.

These were twofold: on Catholicism and on atheism.

Catholics were seen as the national enemy and in the sixteenth century this worked the other way around in Catholic countries, in which Protestants were equally the enemy. In what we now call Germany the rule was '*cuius regio eius religio*', or 'whose kingdom, his religion', which meant that the ruler determined whether or not the country was Protestant or Catholic, and if you as a subject were on the wrong side of what the king or duke chose, then you could be in lethally serious trouble. England was not alone in its policies therefore, and indeed, it was not until 1828 that English Catholics had the same civil rights as the Protestant majority.

Research has now shown that the myth of the English Reformation being a grassroots movement is in fact historical nonsense and the result of successful Protestant propaganda (and perhaps genuine belief by those who held it). Queen Mary Tudor could have, had she lived longer, reimposed Catholicism successfully to England, and the hold of her Protestant half-sister on the throne, Elizabeth, was often tenuous at best. The Queen and her spymasters were well aware of this and, after 1587, when the Catholic claimant to the throne, Mary Queen of Scots, was executed, King Philip II of Spain, who had Lancastrian royal blood as much as the Tudors themselves, decided that he wanted to conquer England for himself and for the Roman Catholic Church. The Pope had decreed that Elizabeth was illegitimate and that all true Catholics in England should want her deposed, and the plotting to murder Elizabeth continued throughout her reign and, indeed, up until the end of it.

This meant, therefore, that *the religious and the political were always enmeshed*, in just the same way in which state loyalty and ideology were in the 1930s. During the latter, if you were a communist you supported the USSR over your own country. It was the same for many devoted Catholics in sixteenth century England. For them, loyalty to the Pope and to Catholic monarchs such as Philip II of Spain was more important than loyalty to your English home country. Although William Allen and other Catholic spies in the sixteenth century would have argued the same as Kim Philby did in the twentieth – that they were being the *true* patriots. They wanted to see England return to the Catholic faith in their time, much as Philby wanted Britain to be communist in his.

So to be a Catholic, however quiet or low key, in Cambridge in the 1580s was as dangerous as being a Bolshevik in the same place in the 1930s, since your ideology automatically meant that you were loyal to an ideology outside your own country in a way that your beliefs automatically rendered you a traitor.

And further, the idea that you could believe in nothing at all – atheism – was regarded as unacceptable to everyone; not until well into the eighteenth century was such thinking even tolerated in Britain.

Finally, you could be a Protestant but of the wrong kind – the Puritans here being the best example. Indeed it was the persecution of Puritan *Protestants* by their *fellow Protestants* in the state Church of England that, as we all know, led to the founding of the colonies in England in the New World such as Massachusetts. This emigration began not long after Marlowe was murdered as the result of one kind of Protestant persecuting another.

So what was Marlowe?

The likelihood is that he fell into the atheist category, or was for certain the kind of person for whom the traditional interpretations of Christian faith were not acceptable. This is possibly what killed him in the end, since his link to the circle of the famous explorer (and co-founder of Virginia) Sir Walter Raleigh, against whom the same accusation was made, tarred him with the same brush as the risky views of this group, which was sometimes known by the soubriquet of the 'School of the Night'.

And here we have to remember that in dealing with the sixteenth century, we are looking at a world whose entire outlook was radically different from our own in terms of the issues that they regarded as important.

But in fact they are not so different – think of the McCarthy era in US politics, where even being thought a communist could brand you a traitor, and indeed of the entire cold war period, in which support for Marxism was often deemed treacherous, since that ideology was the core of the Soviet state, and therefore potentially treasonous.

Perhaps, therefore, the late sixteenth and late twentieth centuries were not so different after all? And think too of being a Muslim student in post-September 11 Cambridge or Harvard. The USA has still to elect an atheist president, so while we think of ourselves as modern, consider too the death toll of Hitler's Germany or Stalin's USSR, and ponder whether we in our time are really any more civilised than those who lived in Elizabethan times.

At some stage during his time at Corpus Marlowe was recruited to work as a spy. We know this because, in March 1587, the Queen's Privy Council put forward an extraordinary resolution asking Cambridge to give Marlowe his MA even though he had been outside residence of Cambridge (an obligation still imposed on its students in the twenty-first century!). It states that he went abroad to do 'her Majestie good service' and that he 'deserved to be rewarded for his faitfull dealings': in other words that he had been abroad as a spy.

However, what exactly had he been up to? The Privy Council notes suggest that he had been in Rheims, which was the headquarters for the Catholic Church's efforts to reconvert England to Roman Catholic faith. Originally in Douai, it moved to Rheims and was the centre of all the plots, both spiritual and political, of William Allen, the eminent Catholic priest in charge of the reconversion effort. As we will see it was thus a source of enormous interest to Walsingham and, indeed, all of Elizabeth's ministers, since it was also a hotbed of plotting to overthrow the Queen and, from the year of the Privy Council note on Marlowe, to substitute someone such as Philip II of Spain on the English throne. (Once again we must remember: the political and the religious were, in this period, exactly the same.)

One of the major theories is that Marlowe had put himself forward as a spy in Rheims itself, and that he was undercover for Walsingham's spy network. There he tried to find out about the priests being smuggled back into England, who were intent not just to give spiritual succour to English Catholics under Protestant yoke but also to act as spies for the Spanish and other Catholic plots to depose Elizabeth and invade England. Indeed, this kind of information was useful in the build-up to the Great Armada of 1588, when Philip's invasion fleet failed, thanks in very large part to Walsingham's spies in the right places.

But was Marlowe one of them? And was he in Rheims?

Most of those who we know for certain went to Rheims were low-key so far as the Catholic hierarchy there was concerned. They were always and very understandably on the lookout for traitors in their midst and aware of Walsingham's attempts to infiltrate them with spies. But surely Marlowe was already too high a profile person to be as anonymous as a good spy should be: he was not as famous as he was soon to become with his plays, but nor was he exactly anonymous either. And the evidence of his time in Cambridge does not suggest that he was pretending to be a Catholic *recusant* and sympathiser – the kind of person from England who would naturally want to attend Rheims – but an atheist, someone who did not actually believe in any kind of Christianity at all. Atheism was as unacceptable to the moral fabric of the nation as Catholicism, albeit not as treasonous. And it was belief in the former that was to face Marlowe at the end of his life. So one would have thought it more likely that his Cambridge notoriety would be of the atheist, rather than of the recusant Catholic, kind.

But it is likely that he was in France, which at that time was engaged in a particularly bloody civil war based ostensibly on who would succeed to the Valois dynasty as King of France, but in practice on religion, a war between conservative Catholics led by the powerful Guise faction (from which Mary Queen of Scots' mother came) and that of the Protestants, the Huguenots, one of whose number, Henry of Navarre, had the best genealogical claim to the French throne. The French Wars of Religion lasted from 1562 to 1598, and ended with Henry becoming a Catholic, to win Paris, but giving French Protestants hitherto unthinkable freedom to worship in 1598. But in 1587 all this was in the future, and what everyone in England remembered was the Massacre of St Bartholomew in 1572, when Catholic gangs, inspired by the Guise, slaughtered thousands of innocent Huguenots in Paris and across France. Sir Francis Walsingham was the English ambassador to France at that time and witnessed the atrocities; the horror that a similar bloodbath could happen in England should the Catholics prevail was constantly in the back of the minds of Elizabeth and her government throughout this period.

Since one of Marlowe's plays was to be about the 1572 massacre, it is quite possible therefore that, even though he was not at Rheims himself, he was in France on Walsingham's behalf in the mysterious and missing 1585–1587 period of his life, during which he was absent from Cambridge and certainly doing something of a political nature for his country. Other key spies, including his fellow Cambridge graduate Richard Poley, were certainly there, as was someone called Richard Baines, another Walsingham agent, who was to have a woeful effect on Marlowe's life. It was Baines' accusations of atheism against him that many feel was to lead to the circumstances of Marlowe's murder in 1593.

From 1587 onwards Marlowe's life is far more documented and less in dispute as to where he was when. The next six years were like that of a meteor flashing briefly but dazzlingly across the skies, since he was to write the plays that would make him permanently famous before being cut down and killed still in his twenties.

Tamburlaine the Great, The Massacre at Paris and *The Jew of Malta* are all plays still studied and read today, as indeed are many of his poems – countless people must have quoted his comment on Helen of Troy's beauty launching a thousand ships without realising who it is that they are quoting.

Up-and-coming at this time, too, was a certain William Shakespeare, who had nothing of the privileged background of Marlowe's Cambridge education. Frustratingly it is impossible to know whether the two theatrical geniuses of their time ever met – it is felt unlikely, alas.

His most notorious play *Dr Faustus* is one of the many renderings of the Faust legend, the most famous being the Goethe operatic version of 1808, but most of which go back to around a few decades before Marlowe's own lifetime and which have German or possibly central European origin.

Marlowe's own version was published posthumously, first performed in 1594 and originally printed a decade later in 1604 (with all sorts of textual difficulties that have perplexed scholars for centuries). His play deals with the eponymous doctor who makes a deal with the devil in order to achieve unlimited knowledge – hence the phrase *a Faustian pact.* The linkage of Marlowe and Faust has long fascinated writers and thinkers including, in more recent times, Herbert Lom, the actor who died in 2012. Famous for his roles in the *Inspector Clouseau* films but, in fact, an intelligent actor of Czech ancestry, Lom at one stage thought of putting together a film on the Faust/Marlowe story. He ended up writing a short book instead, with Marlowe's own life being a Faustian pact in which the forces of darkness and espionage end up killing him in a way that Lom decides not to reveal.

There is much in this notion – one could say that anyone who decides to become a spy makes some kind of Faustian deal or another, especially those who, like the twentieth-century spies in our book, make a pact with their country's enemies. Perhaps Marlowe was speaking from self-knowledge? It cannot be proved but it is an intriguing thought.

Marlowe was a hot-tempered man (which is why the official story of his death in a row over a reckoning or bill has resonance) and in September 1589 he killed a man named William Bradley in a brawl in south London. He was, of course, imprisoned but was lucky to be able to enter a successful plea of self-defence, for which the Queen gave him a pardon, the following year. (Another sign that he was a spy who could not be spared?)

Much of Marlowe's exact whereabouts between his release from jail in late 1589 and his arrest in what was then called the Low Countries (now split between Belgium, the Netherlands and Luxembourg) remains a mystery, which is mysterious in and of itself, as Marlowe, his first plays now performed, was not exactly an unknown person anymore, and suggests that those who attribute this part of his life to espionage are surely on the mark – well-established, up-and-coming playwrights do not just simply disappear...

What we do know is that he was becoming a member of several influential circles, and spent some time as a fellow lodger of another playwright, Thomas Kyd, a man who was himself to get in serious trouble with the authorities for unorthodox views, and whose link with the more famous Marlowe could have been used against the latter, perhaps with fatal results in 1593.

One of these groups was the aforementioned School of the Night, around Sir Walter Raleigh, the great English explorer. He had been a favourite of Queen Elizabeth, but his place in her affections was taken by the young Robert Devereux, Earl of Essex. Essex was a distant cousin of the Queen's through her mother, but perhaps more importantly his godfather and stepfather was Robert Dudley, Earl of

Leicester, the great love of Elizabeth's life. Young Essex was not to prove his stepfather's equal but he certainly wanted to be the most powerful man in England, and this naturally put him at odds with the other groups, notably that of the Cecil family, Elizabeth's greatest supporters and courtiers, and in Marlowe's lifetime the illustrious Lord Burghley, her Lord High Treasurer and his son Sir Robert Cecil, who had by now succeeded Walsingham as Elizabeth's Principal Secretary, and who was to go on to greatness as the ancestor of the Hatfield-based Cecils, still an eminent family in Britain today.

Rivalry as to who was to succeed Elizabeth was rampant – she designated no heir in her lifetime – but the wise odds were on her cousin King James VI of Scotland, son of Mary Queen of Scots but a Protestant, and of descent from Henry VII through his father as well as his mother. We now know him as King James I of the King James Version of the Bible, but back in the 1590s all remained uncertain and murky, with the Spanish threat still present and much intrigue as to who would wield power in the new reign. Essex himself was to play for the ultimate stake, launching a coup in 1601. Foiled by his rivals the Cecils, he paid the ultimate price in being executed for treason. Raleigh too was to die in the Tower of London, another loser in the power stakes, whereas Robert Cecil was to become Earl of Salisbury of Hatfield House and one of the most powerful men in the reign of King James I – a winner.

This is all deemed the background to the espionage that now followed since, with Walsingham dead, each faction had, in effect, their own spy network, all professing loyalty to Elizabeth but, in reality, enemies to each other. So spies were working against other spies, and treachery was afoot.

In 1592 we discover where Marlowe was – in Flushing (proper name Vlissingen) in the Netherlands, then, as now, part of an 80-year war for control between the English-backed, mainly Protestant rebels and the (largely Catholic) defenders of Spanish rule, a foreign domination over what is now Belgium that lasted in that region up to 1815.

Marlowe had been arrested for coining, or illegal counterfeiting. He and his accomplices were sent back to England to face the music there but, so far as Marlowe was concerned, this was only the beginning of his troubles.

For one of those who had reported Marlowe to the authorities was an Englishman, Richard Baines, who was himself some kind of spy. Baines was another Cambridge graduate, this time of Christ's College, and clearly from a wealthy background. He had been one of Walsingham's many recruits at Rheims, the Catholic College, but was clearly not a very good secret agent as his cover had been swiftly blown. Now he was still a spy but in a different faction in the internal power plays of late Elizabethan England, since he was against Marlowe hook, line and sinker. He wrote a booklet-length note on him, denouncing his theological views (or rather, the lack of them), Marlowe's avowed anti-Christian atheism and, rather unlikely in the light of Marlowe's atheism, that the playwright was also an agent of Rome and intended to go over to the enemy there as soon as possible. These accusations were, of course, mutually contradictory but, in a game of destroying one's political opponents by eliminating their underlings, anyone was fair game and Marlowe's outspoken atheism was not exactly a secret.

This being the case, those who wanted to get at Marlowe's patrons could easily find information in their protégé's own life. Raleigh was a major target of the Essex circle, and he was the centre of the School of the Night with its possible links to alchemy and atheism – how better to get at Raleigh than through Marlowe?

By now the noose was also tightening on Marlowe through his former room-mate, Thomas Kyd, best known as the author of the famous Elizabethan play *The Spanish Tragedy*. Kyd was arrested and charged with using lewd or inappropriate language. To protect himself he lashed out at others, implicating Marlowe as a blasphemer who believed that Christ was homosexual.

(This is likely the time of Marlowe's composition of *King Edward II,* which portrays a strongly homoerotic love between Edward II and his favourite Piers Gaveston – whether Marlowe himself was gay has been the source of enormous conjecture but of no firm proof either way.)

Kyd was eventually released, only to die young and in poverty in 1594.

But it was the Baines note that was to cause Marlowe to have to face a summons from the Privy Council in early 1593. And here the conspiracy theories really start to come into their own in a major way, with his murder on 30 May that year. Four men met in a house in Deptford: Christopher Marlowe, Robert Poley (who we have already seen as a major-league spy and linked to Cecil), and two people from the criminal underworld, Ingram Frizer and

Nicholas Skeres, the latter of whom had close ties to the Essex faction.

Christopher Marlowe's death is the sixteenth-century equivalent of who killed Kennedy in 1963, or whether or not Princess Diana's death was an accident. As with all sudden and dramatic events, the controversies have proved to be legion, with each faction often denouncing the other in trenchant terms! In Marlowe's case they also link in with another great centuries-old literary debate: *who wrote Shakespeare?*

Whether or not William Shakespeare wrote his own plays – a recent film put forward the main alternative, the Earl of Oxford as the true author – I think that we can safely cast aside one hypothesis, namely that Marlowe faked his own death and wrote all the rest of his plays under his friend and contemporary Shakespeare's name. Apart from the fact that today most literary scholars now feel that the Bard of Stratford actually composed his own sonnets and plays, the idea that someone as egotistical and publicity-seeking as Marlowe would cede the limelight to someone who was, back in 1593, very much the junior of the two London stage celebrities, is surely far-fetched and distinctly unlikely.

(It is true that Shakespeare did lift a few lines from Marlowe's plays, but that is another matter – many of his history plays lift large amounts from contemporary historians and chroniclers, so a couplet or so from Marlowe does not prove the conspiracy theories to be true.)

So *who killed Marlowe? And why?*

First, the original or official version is sometimes also the true story. It is likely that Princess Diana died in 1997 because she was not wearing a seatbelt. That makes her death still tragic but also rather prosaic. But she was also the 'People's Princess' and real-life people with iconic status do not die prosaically... So despite all the investigations that proved that the dull reason – the lack of a seatbelt – was the true one, we instinctively do not wish to believe it. It could not have been *that* simple, could it?

Or maybe it could.

In which case the official coroner's verdict back in 1593 was indeed correct: Marlowe died in an angry brawl over the 'reckoning', a fight over who would pay that got nasty and out of control, and ended with the death of the most promising playwright of his time. The fact that the three people with him were, like him, also spies, is a coincidence in terms of his actual death. Frizer might have been swiftly pardoned because of his own espionage links (and because he was with an important secret agent such as Poley), *but the actual cause of death was the official one.*

However, when four spies get together and one of them is murdered, and the assailant and two witnesses get pardoned – now that does seem a bit far-fetched, however otherwise convincing the official verdict might suggest. While the obvious or simplest answer is usually the best option, the fact that espionage is heavily involved does make one wonder whether sometimes the conspiracy theory solution is the correct one after all.

But which of the many contradictory stories should one choose? One option has Marlowe being killed on the orders of the Cecil family at court. Yet another has them mourning his loss because he was one of their best agents and about to go on a major secret mission for them that was prevented by his murder. Surely both these conspiracy theories cannot be correct at the same time?

How about his involvement in the School of the Night, the allegedly atheistic circle around Sir Walter Raleigh, the buccaneer and founder of Virginia we saw earlier? Raleigh began a hero and ended his life in the Tower of London. When Marlowe was murdered we know that he was already a marked man with many enemies, the ambitious young Earl of Essex being among them.

Where, too, did the Cecils, old Lord Burghley and young Sir Robert Cecil (the future Earl of Salisbury and ancestor of the Hatfield House Cecils) fit into all this mystery? Did they want Marlowe dead, or was he actually one of their best secret agents in the intrigue in which they were active – who would succeed the increasingly aged and infirm Elizabeth on the English throne?

Occam's razor says that the most obvious answer is the best. But unlike with Diana's seatbelt death we have to reject it, not because Marlowe, like Diana, was a meteoric and popular person cut down too young – though Marlowe, had he lived might have given Shakespeare a competitor – but because he was a spy.

So let us look at some of the rival theories and see which one looks convincing.

Most academics seem to think that his death really was a coincidence, and that exciting theories are just that – speculation. In fact, we did not know what happened for sure at all until the vital missing document, the coroner's report, was found as recently as 1925, over three centuries since his murder. Until then all kinds of speculation had abounded, most of it now proved to be wildly inaccurate, such as that he was killed outside in a street battle rather than inside, with suspiciously few witnesses. The landlady of the tavern, Eleanor Bull, was no low-life serving wench but a very well-connected woman of gentry ancestry with cousins who served at the court. Marlowe did not die in a hovel, therefore, but in an environment that suggests breeding rather than the gutter. And as we saw earlier, Marlowe's temper was notorious, so death by quarrel over a bill is not entirely unlikely. Or is it?

But to me at least the unusual circumstances of his ending make it all the more suspect! This was, therefore, no dingy affair but a meeting in what novels from John le Carré onwards would call a safe-house, a venue in which people from the world of espionage could meet discreetly without prying eyes.

We need therefore to forget academic respectability and discover what those who felt that Marlowe really was murdered, in a possibly pre-ordained way, not killed in a hot flash of sudden rage.

First, some theories to look at and pass by...

Marlowe was one of Sir Francis Walsingham's best spies, and when Sir Francis died that network passed on to Sir Robert Cecil, Walsingham's successor as chief adviser to the Queen, but also someone of significance in his own right as the able and younger son of Lord Burghley, the Queen's faithful Lord High Treasurer. So in 1593 Marlowe is a Cecil man, and nearly all those who have examined the Deptford murder put Marlowe not as an enemy of the Cecils but as their loyal spy and henchman.

Marlowe was murdered in the titanic struggle at the top of Elizabethan society between Sir Robert Cecil, the

Principal Secretary to the Queen, and the wild young new court favourite, the Earl of Essex, Elizabeth's arrogant toyboy, for total power as Queen Elizabeth grew old and her succession uncertain. And as a subplot there is also the deadly rivalry between Essex and a former favourite of the Queen's, Sir Walter Raleigh, in whose circle Marlowe was a key member.

Raleigh was being accused of atheism, and in those religiously paranoid times that could be as much as a capital offence, with atheists being put to death alongside Catholics. For, as we saw at the beginning, the personal was political and religion and politics were all enmeshed in terms of where your ultimate political loyalties lay.

Thus a plot unfolds – Marlowe is close to Raleigh, and Marlowe was an obvious atheist, and if he was, then so too perhaps was Raleigh. And if Sir Walter *was* an atheist, then he was certainly finished at court, and out of the way of the ambitious young Earl of Essex for good.

But at least one book has the Cecils getting rid of Marlowe, because of the poet's involvement with Raleigh and the School of the Night. In this scenario, the Cecils fear what Marlowe knows about them, and have him killed to prevent him from talking.

To me this seems highly unlikely. No one wants to kill one of their best agents, and, in any case, there is no real proof of the claim that the Cecils were closet atheists. It is also the case that they could have had him killed many times over, including abroad, and yet this never happened. The weird and occult world of the School of the Night, as with the parallel dark deeds of the court of mad Emperor Rudolph II in Prague, might be full of fascination, especially post-*Da Vinci Code*, but I do not really see it standing up here.

Nor is there any proof of a gay rationale, even though Marlowe is famous for saying that anyone who did not love both boys and tobacco was lacking in taste: none of the written evidence suggests it.

Having dealt with the unlikely, what claims are more plausible? To me, the best is Charles Nicholl's in his book *The Reckoning: The Murder of Christopher Marlowe*. And to be fair to academics, it is Nicholl who wrote the new official life of Marlowe in *The Oxford Dictionary of National Biography* new edition for the twenty-first century, so his view is not completely outré.

But which version of Nicholl do we take? For the hardback version of his book makes one theory, and the paperback, a few years later, has a quite different theory altogether: one writer and two opinions!

The Nicholl no.1 is that Marlowe got in the way of the deadly Essex-Raleigh rivalry. As he was about to be protected by the Cecils, and therefore expose Essex's plots, he had to be got rid of very quickly before he could give the game away. This is what he would have had to do in order to defend himself against the claims of atheism in which the Essex faction were trying to embroil Raleigh.

So Essex ordered one of his hitmen to get Marlowe out of the way. This was not so much to murder Marlowe, but to discredit Raleigh, and thus remove a popular rival for Essex's consolidation of power over the weak and frail Elizabeth.

And perhaps too – if Marlowe was, as the evidence suggests, indeed a spy for Cecil, then the playwright's death would do no good to the Cecil faction at court either.

Elizabethan politics was a deadly affair, with all sorts of people murdered in mysterious circumstances, with low-life cut-outs such as Nicholas Skeres. Skeres was a crook, con-artist and swindler; the kind of deniable thug that great men like the Earl of Essex used for things that they wanted to happen without the deed being traced back to the person at the top.

Nicholl theory no.1 is, therefore, that Frizer and Ingram colluded to get Marlowe to Deptford, and then do the deed. They are the men in cahoots, and if Robert Poley's presence is suspicious it is because he was present as Cecil's man, not so much to kill Marlowe but to find out what was going on for his master's benefit.

However, those who argue for the Cecil theory – that Lord Burghley and Sir Robert Cecil ordered him dead to cover up their involvement in the School of the Night – point out that a thug like Skeres could have had Marlowe murdered at any time had Essex so wished it. A dark alleyway would have been a better venue than a well-known tavern, especially as someone representing Cecil – Robert Poley – was also present.

And this takes us to another theory, which is that the murder was ordered by Thomas Walsingham, who was ostensibly protecting Marlowe, because the link that Walsingham had was public knowledge and was now becoming embarrassing for him.

This is of course possible – but it might not explain how all three of the very culpable witnesses were pardoned so quickly after the murder. It is nevertheless a plausible alternative that has good backing and that cannot be discounted.

However I tend rather to go for what we might call Nicholl's theory no.2, which is the new one that the author brings out in the much-later paperback edition of his book.

This argues that Marlowe's death was, indeed, still spy-related, and still also tied into the rivalry between the faction of the Earl of Essex and those who might supplant him for power as Elizabeth lay dying.

But in this instance Marlowe's death was a pre-meditated *option* rather than the sole choice and purpose of the meeting. And furthermore, the men at the top of the court conspiracies, the Earl of Essex, Sir Walter Raleigh, Sir Robert Cecil and Lord Burghley, did not necessarily know what their underlings were up to – they heard about it after the fact, which is also a good reason for covering up the murder with well-placed pardons to the guilty.

Now the School of the Night *is* involved, but it is the Raleigh circle that is the target, rather than the Cecils, who, quite rightly, are not, themselves, in any way connected with it. Marlowe is a way of attacking the big fish – Raleigh – rather than being the big fish himself.

Ingram was the man who murdered Marlowe, but it was Skeres, the Earl of Essex's man, who arranged the deed – with Poley, Cecil's man, there primarily to observe. The deal was that if Marlowe agreed to rat on Raleigh and all the atheistic heresies of the School of the Night, when he had to appear before the Council, then he would be left alone. Raleigh would be destroyed and Essex would be triumphant.

But clearly Marlowe refused to agree, not realising that in doing so he was signing his own death warrant. With his rejection of collaboration, of changing sides in the power struggle, he had made himself expendable. And like all people in such circumstances, he could now be disposed of – and was.

The Cecils, according to this view, were appalled, but there was nothing that they could do to bring him back, and so all those involved were pardoned, to live, like Poley, long and prosperous lives.

This theory is the one that makes the most sense to me, given the violent and factional nature of the times. And in my mind it makes Marlowe's death honourable, since he died staying loyal both to his friends and to his beliefs. It does not make it any the less tragic – a genius cut down still in his twenties, a playwright who could, if he had lived longer, have been the equal of his, now more illustrious, contemporary William Shakespeare. Spying is a dangerous game, though, and Marlowe's death proves it. But interestingly, despite that, he is the only one of our Cambridge spies to die violently, maybe proof of how truly brilliant at their craft the others turned out to be.

THE WATCHER
FRANCIS WALSINGHAM

'The past is another country – they do things differently there.' These lines, from playwright Harold Pinter's screen adaptation of the LP Hartley novel *The Go-Between*, have become legendary, and are probably also frequently taken out of context.

But for us they are an essential reminder of how people thought in radically different ways to us in the past. So much so that although, to take Elizabethan England as an example, they speak a form of English to which we are all familiar through Shakespeare or Marlowe, we forget that what mattered to them is very different from what would be important for us today.

But for the chapter on Sir Francis Walsingham, I think that a better analogy could be given – Britain in 1939 to 1940, under threat of foreign invasion, and from a power that wished to undo all that the British people, and certainly their leaders, held most dear. In this I am not original – other writers such as Stephen Alford in his excellent book *The Watchers* have argued the same. (I have followed Alford's title in the name I have given to this chapter.) Likewise Derek Wilson, in his very sympathetic biography (*Sir Francis Walsingham: Courtier in an Age of Terror*) has drawn even more recent parallels, with the threat posed in Elizabethan England from Spain and from the extremist Guise faction in France's 'Wars of Religion' in the 1580s to the equally existential danger posed by terrorism after September 11 in our own time.

All this background is important, since what we are about to read might seem somewhat strange or even alien to us in the twenty-first century. But if we think of it in terms familiar to present-day concerns, or the dire possibility of Nazi conquest in 1939 to 1940 that many still alive remember all too vividly, then perhaps we can grasp better how people thought and reacted back in those dark times during which Walsingham held power and did his best to defend his Queen and country, and all the values for which Elizabethan England stood.

Before we go on to look at Walsingham's life in detail we probably need some background to the epic events of his own time, some of which we might be unfamiliar with in English-speaking countries, but which provided the entire context for his own life and actions.

Most of us are familiar with the terrible Thirty Years War, which so devastated Europe from 1618 to 1648, all after his death. So enormous was the carnage that, from then on, Europeans ceased to fight wars based upon religion in the way in which they had been doing for over a century and more.

But the Thirty Years War was the climax, and we all too often know nothing of those that went before. The first was the overlapping Eighty Years War (from 1568 to 1648), between Spain and those in the Netherlands wanting to gain political and religious freedom from Spanish oppression. Secondly, there were the French Wars of Religion. The latter was a truly savage civil war raging in France 1562 to 1598, between the Huguenots (or Protestants) on the one hand and the ultra-religious Catholic faction led by the Guise family on the other, with the actual kings of France often pawns in a wider struggle.

And in both of these England was, in fact, deeply involved, with English troops fighting in the Netherlands, including Walsingham's own son-in-law, the famous poet Sir Philip Sidney losing his life in the conflict, and Elizabeth's famous 'Sea Dogs' like Sir Walter Raleigh and Sir Francis Drake taking an active part in the naval war against Spain. For all that Queen Elizabeth was keen to keep England out of the wider conflict, other forces were forever dragging her back in, and the Great Armada of 1588, when the Spaniards so dramatically failed to invade and conquer the country, is part of a lengthy Europe-wide struggle for supremacy lasting for most of her reign.

Finally, we come to Elizabeth's cousin, Mary Queen of Scots. Here the two wars – the Eighty Years War and the Wars of Religion – are inexorably bound up in the relationship between the two women, and the struggle for who would rule France. Mary had first been married to a French king, and it was the certainty that the Valois dynasty that had ruled France for centuries would become extinct that helped spark the conflict there. For in the same way as Mary was a Catholic heiress to the English throne, Henry of Navarre was a Protestant (Huguenot) heir to the French throne. And Mary's mother, who was a member of the ultra-Catholic Guise family, was determined to keep the French throne Catholic. In this they had a firm ally – Philip II, King of Spain, and one of the powerful Habsburg family that, under his father Emperor Charles V, had ruled Europe from Spain and the Netherlands to Austria and Hungary and much more besides.

So who controlled England could mean winning power in France and ruling the Netherlands, the latter being a part of Europe that was, in the next century, to create one of the most powerful commercial empires that the world has ever seen.

Sir Francis Walsingham, Elizabeth's Principal Secretary, was therefore not just helping to determine whether or not England stayed free and independent, but who would emerge as the most powerful country in the world. For, as many an Elizabethan pirate discovered, Spain was the wealthiest nation on earth, and that vast fortune came not from its own soil but from Spanish control over the whole of South America (and after 1580 that means *all* of it, since Portugal and its great colony Brazil fell to Philip II's conquering armies that year).

What is amazing is that, against such enemies, England survived at all! And much of that delivery from invasion and tyranny is due to Sir Francis Walsingham, and his network of spies...

He was born at some date in 1532, from an eminent family that had both court connections and, via marriage, links to Elizabeth I herself. His father, William Walsingham, was a prosperous Kent landowner, and his mother Joyce Denny had some very important family. This included her father, Sir Edward Denny, who was one of the key courtiers of King Henry VIII who managed to ensure the Protestant succession in 1547 to Edward VI and that the avowedly Protestant Duke of Somerset would be Lord Protector.

More significantly, when William Walsingham died in 1534 his widow remarried, to Sir John Carey, whose brother William Carey was the husband of Mary Boleyn, Anne Boleyn's sister and of course therefore the aunt of Francis Walsingham's future employer, Elizabeth I. Such ties might seem tenuous in the twenty-first century, but in the sixteenth they were very important and were to be of huge later help to Walsingham as he sought a career for himself.

He became a Cambridge student, and therefore eligible for our book, in 1538, as a Fellow Commoner (or privileged student) of King's College, Cambridge. The college is famous now, as then, for its magnificent chapel, known to this day by millions of tourists from around the world and one of Cambridge's most iconic landmarks. The Provost then was Sir John Cheke, one of the most eminent classical scholars of his time, who also served first as a tutor to the young Prince Edward and, after the Prince's accession, as a Secretary of State to King Edward VI. Significantly, one of his pupils was William Cecil, later Lord Burghley, who married Cheke's sister Mary. Cecil became Elizabeth I's Principal Secretary of State in 1553 and it was his retirement from that office to become Lord Treasurer (as Lord Burghley) that created a vacancy eventually filled by Francis Walsingham himself. Again, connections (and in this instance, the University of Cambridge) made all the difference.

Walsingham did not finish his degree, but went on, as did many young gentlemen of that time, to read for the bar. In his case he chose Gray's Inn, one of the four still existing Inns of Court for barristers.

But his initial career was cut short by the accession to the throne of Mary Tudor as Queen Mary I. As we saw in the last chapter, England lurched from being theoretically Protestant under King Henry VIII, zealously Protestant under his son King Edward VI, and now equally profoundly Roman Catholic again under Mary I. Like many Protestants, Walsingham fled abroad – a wise course as thousands of his fellow believers were burned to death under Mary's active persecution policy of restoring Catholicism and extirpating what she believed to be heresy from her realm.

Many Protestant exiles surprisingly went to Padua, in what we now call Italy, supposedly the heartland of the Roman Catholic faith, but in practice protected from persecution by the Republic of Venice, for whom such zeal was unacceptable. Then, like countless supporters of the Puritan version of Reformation theology, the young Walsingham found himself in Switzerland, much of which was actively Protestant, including the great Swiss city of Basel.

By 1559 Elizabeth had been on the throne a year, and had restored Protestant Christianity back as the official religion of England. Walsingham had made some key connections while overseas, and as a result of one of these he was elected an MP to the House of Commons. He was not what one could call a full-time parliamentarian, but he was to remain one for much of the rest of his life.

His first marriage in 1562 was to Anne Carleill, a wealthy widow (whose son Christopher was to become one of Elizabeth's most active Sea Dogs in many an exciting adventure backed financially by his loving Walsingham stepfather). But she died in 1564 and in 1566 he made his great love match in marrying Ursula Worsley, another rich widow, by whom he had two daughters, Frances and Mary. Here, too, connections would help. Frances married the great Renaissance poet and soldier, Sir Philip Sidney and Sidney was, in turn, the nephew of the great love of Elizabeth's life, Robert Dudley, Earl of Leicester, who will also feature prominently in this chapter. And Ursula Walsingham and Leicester were themselves related.

For a while Walsingham was able to live the life of a country gentleman. But such an existence could not satisfy so able and active a man, and by the late 1560s he was already in touch with Cecil on issues of key policy.

One of these was about Scotland, and here a brief digression is needed to explain the background.

Catholics did not recognise the legitimacy of Elizabeth's birth, especially as it was Henry's marriage to her mother Anne Boleyn that sparked the events that led to the Protestant Reformation in England. To them the rightful heiress of Mary Tudor was her cousin Mary Queen of Scots, who was also a granddaughter of King Henry VII, but unlike Elizabeth, a loyal Roman Catholic. Therefore, as far as many of the Catholic monarchs of Europe were concerned, such as

King Philip II of Spain, and also the Pope, Elizabeth was a heretic, a usurper and illegitimate. Mary of Scotland was the true Queen of England and also the person who would restore what they felt to be the one true faith to that realm.

(As we know, Mary's son, King James VI of Scotland, did indeed succeed Elizabeth to the English throne in 1603, as King James I – but as a Protestant, something that could not have been known by anyone back in the 1560s when his Catholic mother sat on the Scottish throne.)

To us such religious zealotry seems alien. But remember the last chapter – the *personal is political and religion is both.* To Protestants in England, Roman Catholicism was associated with the national enemy Spain – Mary Tudor had been married to her cousin Philip, now King of Spain – and with the massacres that took place during her reign. To be Catholic, therefore, was not just to be different but also to want the overthrow of Elizabeth and the restoration of a religion associated with death and foreign tyranny.

Indeed, just as Walsingham began his official career in 1570, the Pope, Pius V, issued the decree *Regnans in Excelsis.* This not merely said that Elizabeth was illegitimate and a heretic, but that all Catholics who did not work actively for her overthrow would also be excommunicated (or spiritually expelled) from the Roman Catholic Church. So, for English Catholics, a terrible dilemma now arose: support the Queen and be excommunicated, or work for her deposition and risk being executed as a traitor.

And this is the context in which we must see the events that follow. To be Catholic was to be a traitor, and England's enemies were the Catholic powers of Europe, especially the superpower of the sixteenth century, Spain. This was at the background of the minds of all Elizabeth's courtiers, and, because of his own beliefs and experiences, especially that of Francis Walsingham. In his biography, Derek Wilson's excellent understanding of Walsingham's theological thinking helpfully makes this very clear for modern readers.

In 1570 he began his ascent of the ladder by being appointed English ambassador to France. Here he was immediately involved in two of the key issues of the time. The first was the issue of whom Elizabeth would marry. Linked with this were the French Wars of Religion. These questions were entwined for many years to come.

Elizabeth, as we now know, wisely chose never to marry. She could easily have died in childbirth as, for example, did Jane Seymour, mother of King Edward VI – such an event in those medically unsafe times was no respecter of rank. Any husband would immediately become powerful and at the expense, almost certainly, of his wife. England had only had one previous queen regnant (or ruling queen) and Elizabeth's half-sister Mary was not the best precedent.

Elizabeth probably knew this in some way or another, always left unspoken. But her politicians did not, and to them the only way for her to continue the Tudor dynasty was for her to marry and have children. So, for much of her reign, there was an endless to-ing and fro-ing between the Queen and the political classes on this very issue, and for many years the prime candidate for Elizabeth's hand were the two last Valois brothers, confusingly both called Duke of Anjou at different times. Both were years younger than Elizabeth and, like all the doomed Valois, all were to die childless, a factor that increased the ferocity of the Wars of

Religion in France since the heir, Henry of Navarre, was a Protestant.

Much of Walsingham's time was to be taken up with foreign affairs until his death in 1590. At least one of his biographers, Derek Wilson, feels that, therefore, it is anachronistic to call him a spymaster. His reason is that Walsingham's main job on returning from France was to be the equivalent of two modern-day jobs. The first is the Secretary to the Cabinet (a Civil Service post). The second is Foreign Secretary (or Secretary of State in the USA.) Walsingham was, in effect, both of these rolled into one.

In many ways this is true. But given the times in which Walsingham lived, to see him also as the sixteenth century equivalent of Head of both MI6 and MI5 is also true, since without spies he could not have done his job properly, especially as the dangers of invasion from Spain from the outside, and Catholic plots from the inside, got worse as the 1580s progressed. And being a spymaster is – contrary, I feel, to what Derek Wilson writes – certainly no slur.

The ins and outs of Elizabeth's foreign policy are very complex, and are best suited to a more general book than this one. Suffice it to say here that Walsingham did his best for English interests, for both national security and for trade, during his time in Paris. But then, in August 1572 came one of the most notorious and dreadful mass murders in the history of Europe, known as the St Bartholomew's Massacre of 23rd and 24th of that month. Henry of Navarre, the Protestant Huguenot leader, in a move aimed at peace, married Margaret of Valois, the Catholic sister of the French king. But the faction of the Guise family (from which Mary Queen of Scot's mother came) instigated the murder of the main Huguenot leader, Admiral Coligny, and the resulting massacre of the many Huguenots in Paris for the wedding led to the slaughter of over 2,000 of them in Paris alone, and upwards of 10,000 more butchered throughout the rest of France.

Walsingham was very brave throughout this terrifying time, doing all he could to protect English Protestants in Paris from being murdered by the mob, and trying – alas in vain – to safeguard the lives of several Huguenots as well. While he was to go on to support Queen Elizabeth in the endless negotiations with the Valois dynasty over the next decade, his distrust of Catholicism and of the House of Guise and their ally King Philip II of Spain was to remain.

In 1573 he returned from Paris and was appointed to the post that he held the rest of his life, Principal Secretary to the Queen, which, as we have just seen, merged several modern posts in one, on 20th December 1573, and was sworn in as a privy councillor the next day.

For over three centuries the Privy Council has been an essentially honorific office. It meets weekly but in practice it is the Prime Minister (and the Cabinet) who effectively run the Queen's (or King's) government. But in Elizabethan times the Privy Council, the inner circle of advisers to the sovereign, took the crucial decisions, in theory acting as counsellors to the Queen but in reality, as Elizabeth was a major procrastinator, actually ruling on her behalf.

(It was fascinating, in carrying out the research for this chapter, to discover from so many of the more recent historical studies, quite how indecisive Elizabeth I was and how far removed she was from the carefully stage-managed Gloriana of propaganda and national myth.)

Again, much of what Walsingham was doing was complex foreign policy and need not detain us here. But what is interesting is that modern thinking on Elizabethan England stresses how thoroughly *unsafe* she was on her throne for most of her reign, and certainly from her accession in 1558 down to three decades later and the defeat of the Spanish Armada in 1588. Her tenure of the throne was very fragile and her security, internally and externally, could never be guaranteed.

This is why, to me, Walsingham was not just the equivalent of the Head of MI6 (the Secret Intelligence Service, with spies outside the country) but also that of MI5, the Security Service, guarding the country against internal threats as well. I think that Derek Wilson's analogy of the post-September 11 terrorist threat is an apposite one, since the dangers to Elizabeth of Catholic terrorism never really went away, and was a source of endless worry to her counsellors, especially to Walsingham, whose responsibility it was to prevent any plots from being successful.

One of his greatest threats was Mary Queen of Scots, who had fled Scotland in 1568, having been deposed as Queen in favour of her infant son James. As we saw earlier, Mary was a massive threat to Elizabeth. She was Catholic, she had a male heir and after 1570 she was the candidate of all Catholics overseas for the English throne, and, as Walsingham knew, that of many English Catholics as well.

Nowadays we find religious persecution of any kind deeply distasteful, and rightly so. In the sixteenth century it was far more complicated, since the form of religion and national identity went so closely together throughout Europe. And as we saw in the Marlowe chapter, Graham

Greene in the twentieth century made the interesting connection between the Catholic underground missionaries to England, sent by William Allen in the sixteenth century, to the Cambridge spies who spied for the NKVD (Soviet secret intelligence, the precursor to the KGB) in Greene's own era. There is much in this analogy, if one substitutes secular ideological belief (Marxist-Leninism) for religious (Roman Catholicism).

Likewise I think that Derek Wilson is right to say that there is also another kind of link, in that the Catholics who plotted to overthrow and murder Elizabeth I during Walsingham's time in office, have parallels with similar religiously-motivated terrorism in our own time, although I think that there would need to be caution on how far one could take that example.

But be that as it may, the main point is that Walsingham had to combat the internal threat that *Regnans in Excelsis* posed to both the Queen and the existence of Protestantism itself in England, and that to do this he had legions of informers to give him the information that he had to have.

In other words, *he needed spies at home as well as abroad.*

And here is why I use the title 'The Watchers' - inspired by Professor Stephen Alford's book – for this chapter. England in the sixteenth century was in many ways as wonderful as the legend of *Merrie England* and of the age of Shakespeare and Elizabeth's wonderful Sea Dogs suggests. But it was also a nation that was permanently insecure, with plots at home and the ever-present threat of Spain abroad (not to mention the possibility of the Guise faction, Mary's relatives, winning in France). As a result it was, to a very large extent, what we would now call a police state. Freedom as we understand it today was certainly not present, and the penalties for going against the Queen, even trivially by modern standards, could be drastically severe, if not frequently fatal.

Over all this presided Sir Francis Walsingham (as he became when he was knighted by the Queen in 1577), and his extensive spy network.

Here one should say that it was not an official security/spy network, since MI5 and MI6 did not exist until the twentieth century, each organisation created in effect in the run-up to the First World War. Cecil, now Lord Burghley, had spies of his own, as did other leading Elizabethan statesmen, and much of the time the costs had to come out of their own pockets, including Walsingham's which, for him, was a hardship as he was nothing like as wealthy as his more eminent colleagues such as Burghley and Leicester.

So far as internal plots were concerned, there was an especial problem. Elizabeth refused, out of monarchical solidarity, to have Mary executed, which she could have commanded at any time. Had she done so it would have made her life much easier. Certainly Walsingham felt that was the case. He and other courtiers groaned at how Mary's presence in various castles over the years made it easy for plotters who wanted to overthrow Elizabeth and substitute Mary as Queen.

Here one can point out that, while Elizabeth continued to be squeamish about executing Mary, her enemies were not so scrupulous. Not only would they have happily had her assassinated – a source of constant worry for Walsingham –

but they did not hesitate to murder their enemies themselves, with William the Silent, Prince of Orange and leader of the rebels in the Netherlands, brutally killed on 10th July 1584, an event that sent shock waves around Europe and made the English realise how high the stakes were for which they were playing.

But thanks to the developing science of cryptography, Walsingham was able to have a very good idea of Mary's plots and with whom she was conspiring, whether she was the instigator or not. Here he was much aided by one of the first cryptanalysts, Thomas Phelippes, who soon became one of the key members of Walsingham's staff. Phelippes, like some of the later spies in this book, was a graduate of Trinity College, Cambridge, and so expert did he become at code breaking that, as one author has put it, sometimes he would know more about a plot than the plotters themselves.

One of their best spies was in the French Embassy in London – a similar situation to the happy one hundreds of years later when MI6 had Oleg Gordievsky as a key agent inside the Soviet Embassy, when he was able to brief both Mikhail Gorbachev and Margaret Thatcher at the same time!

Of the many plots foiled by Walsingham with Phelippe's technical aid, two are worth mentioning. The first is the Throckmorton plot of 1582, in which a plot involving the Spanish ambassador, Catholic exiles, France and some key English nobles to put Mary on the throne, was uncovered thanks to some excellent detective work by Walsingham's agents.

And here is a classic dilemma of espionage. With the spy in the French Embassy providing so much good information, Walsingham had a problem. Mendoza, the Spanish ambassador was expelled, but Mauvissière, the French ambassador, was not, though he was equally culpable. Surely, historians now speculate, this is because if the French ambassador was thrown out, his secretary would go with him and thus an essential source of English intelligence would be lost. Better to keep the agent in place with his boss than lose an insight into what the enemies of the country were plotting.

All this, as throughout the chapter, comes against the background of the French Wars of Religion and of the Eighty Years War between the Netherlands and Spain – with the active support for King Philip II of Spain for the hardline, ultra-Catholic Guise faction in the French wars providing the common link. England was involved in helping the Dutch in their struggle for freedom. This was for political reasons for many people, such as the Queen herself who valued her own survival understandably highly, and for others such as Walsingham and the Earl of Leicester, it was for overtly religious Protestant reasons.

And after 1586 Leicester also became commander of the English forces in the Netherlands – with his lack of military skill it was not an ideal appointment – and England was thus even more involved in the affairs of continental Europe than it had been before. In all this Walsingham, as Principal Secretary, played a vital role.

The Throckmorton plot uncovered an international conspiracy, and, here too, Walsingham's spy network, which was pan-European, proved absolutely essential to English security. England was nowhere near as powerful then as Spain, which was the superpower of its era, and an invasion would be very easy to complete once Spanish troops actually landed on English soil. The key thing was either to prevent such an invasion from happening at all, or, should it be launched, to defeat it at sea, since the Royal Navy was the one part of the country's armed forces that really punched well above its weight.

(Indeed as Hugh Bicheno has so ably explained in his exciting *Elizabeth's Sea Dogs*, the Royal Navy in the 1580s really was world class, which, given the threat of Spanish seaborne invasion, was just as well.)

Walsingham was involved in the maritime fight against Spain in many ways. He helped to subsidise many of Sir Francis Drake's famous expeditions against Spanish territory in the New World, against their ships carrying vast treasures from Latin America across the Atlantic, and in Drake's spectacular attacks on the Spanish fleet in harbour in Spain itself – as Drake would put it, singeing the King of Spain's beard.

Drake's bravery and that of Elizabeth's other legendary Sea Dogs were ultimately, though, only able to buy time. However strict the security around Mary, there was always someone somewhere who aimed to make her the focus of a plot to murder Elizabeth. And with the ultimate plotter being King Philip II of Spain and his Guise allies in France, the internal threat and the danger of foreign invasion were increasingly enmeshed in what was now called 'the Enterprise of England'.

Thanks to Phelippes, a link was found in 1586 between Mary, now under secure house arrest in Essex, and Anthony Babington, an English Catholic plotting to assassinate Elizabeth. Walsingham now had the killer evidence he needed to show that, not only was there a massive threat to England's safety, but also that Mary was profoundly implicated in the plots to murder her English cousin. Elizabeth's many years of prevarication would soon have to end.

Walsingham had his success. Mary was taken to Fotheringay Castle in Northamptonshire in October 1586, put on trial and found guilty at a more formal proceeding in London, in which Walsingham played a part as one of the key witnesses to Mary's treachery. Although Elizabeth protested, in the end she was outmanoeuvred by her courtiers and on 8th February 1587 Mary was finally executed back at Fotheringay.

Elizabeth put on an outward show of great wrath, since she was understandably nervous that she had created a precedent for executing fellow sovereigns. Fortunately for Walsingham he was absent from court during her storm of vitriol, and for a sad reason. His son-in-law, the great and brave poet Sir Philip Sidney, had been killed at the siege of Zutphen in October 1586, sadly leaving behind him a young family and massive debts, which his not at all wealthy father-in-law now had to assume for himself. (Walsingham's biographers are surely right in their unanimous agreement that Elizabeth's ingratitude to Walsingham, and to Sidney's memory, in not cancelling or aiding this vast debt burden was not an act befitting a Queen, especially as Walsingham and his spies had unquestionably saved her life over many years.)

Mary's death now changed the European equation. Mary had been the Catholic heir to the English throne, but with her execution, the plotters did not want to put her

Protestant son King James VI in her place. Philip II had remote Lancastrian descent from John of Gaunt, and so he became a possible King himself, although most historians now think that he would have placed one of his daughters on the throne instead and found a suitable husband for her. Whoever is right – and there is no scholarly agreement – the invasion of England now took on a new dimension since there was no Mary to substitute for Elizabeth.

Drake had bought some time for his country but spies were now needed all over Europe since the Enterprise of England was very much under way. And Walsingham was under no illusion as to what would happen if Spanish-controlled troops actually landed – as he told Leicester late in 1587, unless God came to the rescue: 'we cannot long stand'.

So now Walsingham's international spy network really came into its own, since although the fleet sailed from Spain, the actual army itself was under the command of the Prince of Parma in the Spanish-ruled part of the Netherlands. The idea was that the fleet would gain control of the English Channel and then the invasion barges, carrying the troops, would be able to cross and land in England for the actual military part of the invasion itself. Fortunately Walsingham's spies were everywhere – in Spain, in Paris and also in Venice, since Italian merchants were a major source of international news, and in the Netherlands as well.

Here I agree with writers who use a different analogy from Graham Greene's cold war/Catholic exiles picture, of 1930s NKVD agents being similar to the Catholic priests being smuggled into England. It is certainly true that the intellectual leader of the Catholic exiles, William Allen, whose importance was recognised by his elevation by the Pope to the rank of cardinal, now unleashed a whole slew of propaganda, denouncing Elizabeth as illegitimate, heretical and many other things besides, in a way designed to pave a path for the future reconversion of England should the invasion be successful.

But other writers see parallels with England in 1940, a possible invasion from Nazi Germany imminent and more than likely. In the same way as RAF Fighter Command saved Britain that year in the Battle of Britain, so too could one argue that the Royal Navy, under Lord Howard of Effingham, fulfilled the same function of saving England from Spain in 1588. And since the Home Guard would not have stood long against the German Wehrmacht in 1940, it is equally unlikely that the troops that Elizabeth inspected at Tilbury in 1588 would have lasted against the experienced and battle-hardened *tercios* in Flanders awaiting the signal for attack.

Walsingham did not have the 1580s equivalent of Bletchley Park, the place where the British, with help from Polish exiles, were able to break the German codes during the Second World War. But they did have several well-placed agents that were able to give an accurate account of the progress of the Armada fleet towards England, and some have argued that, in fact, Walsingham almost had too much information, which made sorting the vital intelligence from the dross hard to accomplish.

Copious amounts of books have been written about the Armada and its failure in the summer and autumn of 1588 to achieve its purpose. The bravery of Sir Francis Drake and others has become legendary, and indeed, the narrow escape of England from what seemed to be inevitable defeat has become an iconic moment in what Churchill called our island story, a victory that is indeed paralleled really only by his similar win against Nazi Germany, against the odds, in 1940.

Much has been attributed to the weather, which wreaked havoc against the Spanish ships. But more recently some historians, most notably Hugh Bicheno in *Elizabeth's Sea Dogs* have argued that English naval tactics played an equally pivotal role, something important to note since the Spanish Armada was far larger than the Royal Navy and, on paper at least, far more powerful. While ours is not a naval history book, the story told by Bicheno and others is compelling, and pays due tribute to the very high and possibly superior quality of English seamanship in relation to that of the Spanish invaders.

By 1589 Walsingham was very ill – he had never really been in good health, with what we would now describe as long-term kidney-stone disease – and he had to spend much of that year at home, unwell. He was actively involved in foreign policy (and what post-September 11 is called homeland security) right up until his death on 6th April 1590. He had served his country well, as well as his ungrateful Queen, and the creation of cryptography and an international spy network was a major part of his achievement.

PART 2

There were surely spies educated at Cambridge in the seventeenth to nineteenth centuries. But in this book, Part 2 will concentrate on those who were at the University in the twentieth, and especially those who attended it as students in the 1930s. Five of them became notorious but, as we shall discover, there were far more than just five of them...

PORTRAIT OF A SPY
Anthony Blunt

What did we know and when did we know it? That is often asked about investigations or cover-ups or other crimes and mysterious episodes, and the story of Anthony Blunt is a classic example of this genre. Famous for most of his life for being one of the world's leading art historians - the global authority on the artist Poussin - he suddenly, aged 72, became infamous for reasons less to do with aesthetics or his decades of scholarship, but for being outed, in public as a gay man (a secret long known to artistic circles but not to a wider audience), and as someone who had been a spy for the Soviet Union for over a decade. He was to be the Fourth Man uncovered in the notorious Cambridge spy ring: first Burgess and Maclean in 1951 when they fled to the USSR, then Philby when he did the same in 1963, and now Blunt in London, in 1979. A private man, he was now exposed very publicly; his lifelong secrets open to scrutiny for the first time.

Blunt is interesting in many ways, since his story is both intellectually fascinating but also misleading. In that what we *now* know, with the defection to Britain of Oleg Gordievsky, and also with the publication of the authorised history of MI5 by Christopher Andrew, is very different indeed from what we *thought* we knew. Especially back in 1979, when Blunt's past as an NKVD spy was brought out into the open by Andrew Boyle's book *The Climate of Treason*, and what had been darkly guarded and secret became what we thought was public knowledge, but not in fact the truth. For as Christopher Andrew has written, the interpretation by rogue hardliners and conspiracy theorists *within* MI5, because of the Blunt case, perhaps did even more damage to British intelligence, and to the Security Service, MI5, in particular, than anything Blunt did in his own years as an NKVD spy in Britain. With Blunt the conspiracy theorists have a field day, and it is only now that we know the *actual* truth that we can write about both him and his circle properly.

So far so mysterious! Let us see, therefore, why Blunt is so interesting as a spy and why what should be straightforward has been so much misinterpreted for many years...

He was born on 26 September 1907, which makes him the oldest of the Magnificent Five of the key Cambridge spies. He was born at home in a vicarage in the deeply traditional British seaside town of Bournemouth, where his father, the Rev Stanley Blunt, was the Vicar of Holy Trinity. While his father was a clergyman, the Blunts were related to the infamous nineteenth century dissenter, journalist and campaigner Wilfred Scawen Blunt, so one could say that

Anthony Blunt was from the respectable side of a raffish family. For some of the time his father was Chaplain to the British Embassy in Paris, so Blunt, as a child, had first-hand experience of France, on whose art, especially of the eighteenth century, he was to become one of the foremost experts.

Blunt was educated at Marlborough School, now famous principally for being one of the first private schools to admit girls as full pupils (Philby's Westminster being another) and for Kate Middleton, now Duchess of Cambridge, as the most famous Old Marlburian. He was not happy there, and it was at school, as with so many boys at boarding schools of his time, that he discovered his homosexuality. For most boarders it is a phase which they change from on meeting girls when older (and now girls at their own school) but for Blunt it was a permanent orientation, as with his brother, the art teacher Wilfred JW Blunt, who for decades was to teach the subject at Eton.

Blunt's closest friend there was the poet Louis MacNeice – the MacNeice-Blunt correspondence has proved a goldmine for biographers and historians, including for Miranda Carter, author of the main life of Anthony Blunt (which is invaluable but written before Christopher Andrew's official history of MI5). Blunt and MacNeice were what was then called aesthetes: artistically inclined rebels against the rather oppressive and distinctly philistine predominant culture of their day. And here it should be said that an aesthete was by no means inevitably gay – some like Blunt were, others were bisexual and others still, like MacNeice, were straight. There are many clichés about people of this time, and we cannot put them all neatly in a single box – for example, the only traitor in their midst was Blunt, and while many of them rejected conformity, betraying your country was not something that would have occurred to any or certainly most of them.

Blunt went up to Trinity College, initially and, perhaps surprisingly in view of his artistic leanings, to read mathematics. Trinity was, in fact, globally renowned for its science – as we saw it is a college that has more Nobel Prize winners than France – and the Master during his time, Sir JJ Thompson, was one such distinguished scientist, in his case with a Nobel Prize in Physics. And as we shall see in a later chapter, there was plenty of espionage going on in the scientific community, both of a clandestine kind but also fairly overt, with leading Soviet scientists spending academic time at Cambridge and openly bringing the key discoveries that they made back to the USSR.

None of this was within Blunt's purview, however, since his interests were taking him in different academic directions. To his intense disappointment he achieved only a second in Mathematics in the first exams (the equivalent of a 2:1 today), and so made what turned out to be the wise decision to switch to modern languages, eventually gaining the longed-for first class honours in both German and French. Art History in those days was not an academic discipline in Britain, which still had a rather old-fashioned and snobbish attitude to making it a subject of proper study and scholarship. In becoming a *de facto* art historian and connoisseur Blunt was ahead of his time, a pioneer, moreover someone middle class in an area that was still dominated by rich or aristocratic gentleman amateurs such as Kenneth Clark, whose vast inherited textile wealth enabled him to study art abroad in a way that was impossible for those from less *comparatively* privileged scholars like Blunt.

While male homosexuality remained illegal in Britain until the 1960s, at Cambridge, still a bastion of the privately-educated from boarding schools, it was, while not prevalent, certainly not uncommon. After the sorrows of his first year, Blunt was able to discover many things, and his sexuality and the ability to practise it was among them.

Here we come again into the realm of myth-making in relation to the spies of the 1930s. As we see in the chapter on Burgess and Maclean, Guy Burgess, the old Etonian at Trinity College, was openly and promiscuously gay. But of the 'Five' he was the only one like that. Blunt's homosexuality was, like Blunt himself, more inward and introspective, and of the Five only Blunt and Burgess were exclusively gay, with Maclean being predominantly heterosexual and occasionally gay, and Philby and Cairncross being very decidedly heterosexual, along with the spies whom Blunt himself recruited – Michael Straight and Leo Long. The idea of a 'homintern' to go along with the Soviet 'Comintern' is ridiculous and misleading, as well as being an excuse for homophobia, since many of the young communists who died in Spain, for instance, were entirely heterosexual, and leading Cambridge homosexuals, such as John Maynard Keynes, fully patriotic and not pro-Soviet or in favour of treason in any shape or form.

It is true, however, that since homosexuality was illegal, many gay men, of whom Blunt was one, got used to living compartmentalised lives – hence the apt title of Miranda Carter's biography *Anthony Blunt: His Lives*. As Carter has observed, while most people in academic and artistic / aesthetic circles knew that Blunt was gay – in such company it was not exactly secret – since it was against the law he was circumspect, and tried deliberately not to behave in the clichéd way that he rather despised but was also one that others would regard as stereotypical. Therefore, in his case, the double life that spies had to lead – outwardly loyal to their country but secretly agents for the other side and traitors – was one to which he was already accustomed. But since Philby and Cairncross of the Five and Leo Long (as well as others such as the atomic bomb spy Klaus Fuchs), also led double lives as spies and were heterosexual, one cannot always make the parallel that many people do when writing about the Cambridge spies.

Kim Philby enjoyed being an NKVD agent because he saw it as being part of an elite, the best espionage network that anyone could be asked to join. At Cambridge Blunt was already part of the elite of the elite – he was invited to be one of the Apostles, the secretive debating society, mainly of Trinity College and King's College students and graduates, which stretched back into the nineteenth century and still exists, albeit in very different form, today.

Here again there are many myths!

Conspiracy theorists *love* secret societies, from the Freemasons through to the Skull and Bones club at Yale. All sorts of amazing and *deeply* secret and thus profoundly conspiratorial things are supposed to happen at them! Dark and clandestine plots to rule the world, to control the global economy, to put the UN in charge of the universe... all these are attributed in some way or another to secret societies and the Apostles is no exception.

Today they are often economists, and back in the 1930s one of the greatest economists of all time (depending upon your point of view), John Maynard Keynes, was among them – a leading Apostle and also the Bursar of King's College. Not only was Keynes a radical economist but he was also gay (though like many of his time, officially married to a Russian ballerina) and strongly connected to the main aesthetic movement of the time, the Bloomsbury Group. With Keynes, therefore, many conspiratorial buttons are all pressed at the same time! However, he was never a Communist, never betrayed his country, and after the Second World War did all he could to achieve for Britain the best economic deal possible with the USA after the financial devastation of the preceding years.

Part of the problem is the phrase of another gay King's College graduate and Apostle, the famous writer EM Forster. Forster once wrote that if he had to choose between betraying his friends or his country, that he hoped he would have the courage to betray his country.

This has in many ways tarred the whole Apostles/Bloomsbury connection, as if all of them were traitors on the basis that two of them – Anthony Blunt and Guy Burgess – were Soviet spies. Certainly the 'Bloomsberries' were notoriously unconventional! Their fanaticism about relationships and their worship of friendship also puts them apart from much of mainstream twentieth-century life. But, however unusual many of their lifestyle choices might have been at the time – today they would probably be seen only as mildly eccentric – they were certainly not traitors in the mould of the Magnificent Five.

And one can also exaggerate their homosexuality – while many of them were gay, or perhaps more accurately gay while effectively celibate, not all of them were, and indeed some were much married and notoriously heterosexual. It is true that some of the aesthetes in their number debated what they called the 'higher sodomy', but in reality that was as much an affectation and a deliberate rebellion against conventional bourgeois morality than anything else – and their heterosexual members offended against the Puritan mores of the day as much as those who were gay. Again, one must remember that the most eminent of the Magnificent Five, Kim Philby, was never an Apostle and was also straight.

But being part of a secret elite *was* important to Blunt, who became an enthusiastic member of the circle of Dadie Rylands (a fellow of King's College from 1927 to 1999), who was both gay and a leading Shakespeare expert, but who, despite also being an authority on the works of Christopher Marlowe, was certainly not a spy, and whose death in 1999 ended the decades-long link between the academic world of Cambridge and the aesthetic/artistic world of Bloomsbury.

During this time Blunt's political views were shifting, against the same backdrop that we have seen with the other Cambridge recruits – the rise of fascism in Europe and Nazism in particular, and the clash between the Soviet and fascist totalitarian world views in Spain. Like Philby he was open, through these events, to the siren call of communism, and thus, in his case as in theirs, to being a Soviet spy.

Blunt's conversion to communism came through his friend and fellow Apostle Guy Burgess, around 1934 to 1935. In writing about this time, one has to remember that as a spy, Blunt was not necessarily telling the truth. But since so many other people in that era converted in similar ways, we do, on this occasion, have no reason to disbelieve him. As he put it later: 'I became convinced that the Marxist interpretation of history was right and that therefore this was where the logical break took place and that one ought to be a communist at that moment. And when Guy put it to me that the best way to help anti-fascism was to help in his work for the Russians, I agreed.'

And as the journalist Phillip Knightley has put it, given the circumstances of the time, how could one not resist the siren call of the fight against fascism? The menace of Hitler, Mussolini – and by 1936 Franco as well – was overwhelming, and the appeasement-dominated and fearful governments in the west were doing nothing to stop the forward march of the totalitarians. The irony is that, in supporting Stalin and the Soviet Union, the young idealists were giving themselves to a regime and ideology every bit as monstrous and oppressive as Hitler and, as Blunt and Burgess were becoming Soviet spies, Stalin was starving over three million peasants to death in the Ukraine.

Then with Blunt, along with Burgess, Maclean, Cairncross and Long, the Nazi-Soviet Pact in August 1939 should have woken them up to the true nature of the regime for which they had decided to spy. But, as with Kim Philby, they passed it over and from September 1939 to June 1941, when the Germans invaded the USSR, they were, in fact, spies for the *de facto* ally of Nazi Germany, for that is precisely what Stalin's Soviet Union was during this period. So much, one could say, for anti-Fascism.

The interesting thing about many of the recruits – in Blunt's case he was to work first with Arnold Deutsch ('Otto') and then with Theo Maly, the Hungarian NKVD illegal and Hungarian exile – is that, as long-term penetration agents, they did not initially have jobs of the kind that would be of any use to the USSR. Maclean and Cairncross, both as civil servants, did of course, but one doubts whether art criticism of the kind now dabbled in by Blunt was of huge help in Moscow, even though, as his writings apparently show, his reverence for the stern creed of Soviet realism become increasingly evident in his articles.

Blunt was, after the war, world famous as an art historian, but his career as one is not our main concern here. Suffice it to say that he ended up at the Courtauld Institute, ironically a part of London University made rich by the very successful and wholly capitalist Courtauld family, whose art collection has proved to be one of the best in the world, and whose understanding of art history as a legitimate academic subject completely transformed the serious study of art in Britain.

In September 1939 war broke out and, thanks to his friends in the capitalist and elite world of Cambridge, Blunt was recruited to work for the Security Service, MI5. His connection was through his university contemporary Victor (later Lord) Rothschild, the scion of the banking dynasty, and himself to be a member of MI5 and one of its bravest officers. This link with Blunt and with Guy Burgess, both of whom lived in a Rothschild-owned apartment during the war, was to cause Rothschild no end of grief in later years and, as we shall see, do his reputation massive damage as many of the more conspiracy-minded members of MI5 found it hard to believe that someone so close to Blunt and Burgess could not himself have been a spy.

Initially Blunt's job was to open the correspondence of neutral, or possibly unfriendly, governments whose embassies were based in London. But as time progressed he became trusted and worked with Guy Liddell, a career officer of MI5 who was eventually to go far in the Security Service.

Here too was someone whose later life was to be ruined by association with the Magnificent Five.

For, in employing Blunt in a sensitive job, Liddell was ignoring the fact that, uniquely out of the Five, as Christopher Andrew puts it, only Blunt was on the suspicious list. He had been to the USSR as a tourist (one of what Lenin had earlier called 'useful idiots') and then had given a lecture to the Marx Memorial Library. When he had tried to join the Intelligence Corps in 1939, he was in fact turned down as unsafe. Yet when Victor Rothschild introduced him to Liddell, the latter became convinced that 'Blunt had never been a communist in the full political sense, even during his days in Cambridge'.

This was, of course, nonsense. But as the American baseball legend Yogi Berra once put it, hindsight is a wonderful thing. This is the case with all the Cambridge spies since, as we saw with Kim Philby, the British establishment of the time seemed incapable of ascribing malign motives to anyone in the ruling classes, and Blunt, while no aristocrat, was from an eminent family and a former fellow of Trinity College. What is obvious now was not so then.

What is extraordinary, though, is that Blunt and the other Cambridge spies were nearly shot by the Russians themselves. Moscow Centre could not believe its luck that by 1941 they were getting vast amounts of information from their spies right at the heart of the British establishment, from Philby in MI6, from their atomic bomb spies, from their moles in Government Communications HQ at Bletchley Park, from Maclean at the Foreign Office – and this not to mention the very highly-placed spies that they also had in the USA, such as Alger Hiss, Harry Dexter White and Klaus Fuchs.

The NKVD was, in fact, so paranoid that they believed not in their good fortune but that this was too good to be true – and therefore was not true. Blunt, Philby and others must all be British double agents and thus traitors to the Soviet cause. In 1942 this was all written up in a Moscow Centre report by NKVD British expert Elena Modrzhinskaya, mainly on the basis that none of the Cambridge spies had revealed the existence of any similar moles or spies in Moscow working for MI6. Blunt's biographer Miranda Carter has commented that the NKVD were, at one stage, so profoundly suspicious because of this that they thought that Blunt, Burgess and Philby should be assassinated. Blunt's death would have been tragic, as he probably did not betray, during this time, the lives of any real British agents anywhere. As Christopher Andrew laconically puts it, this was in fact because there were no British spies in Moscow, partly for the gallant reason that Britain and the USSR, after June 1941, were allies against the Nazis.

Ironically some of this is due to one of the biggest British success stories of the Second World War, in which MI5, Blunt's employers, played a pivotal role. This was the Double Cross System, made famous in the book written later by its presiding genius Sir John Masterman, and by the recent books of Ben Macintyre, such as *Agent ZigZag*. The British, astonishingly but truly were able to find all the Nazi spies in Britain and turn them into double agents working for the British against their German employers, in a deception that proved amazingly successful, and, in relation to deceiving the Nazis on where D-day would be launched, arguably saved thousands of allied lives and maybe even helped to shorten the war.

The Soviets knew about this – through Blunt! But the NKVD, being perpetually paranoid, became convinced that MI6 was playing a similar game with them, and turning the Soviet spies into successful British double agents, as MI5 had done with the German spies working in the United Kingdom. In fact this was not the case, and Blunt, totally loyal to his Soviet masters was, in fact, utterly genuine in his allegiance to them, copying copious amounts of incredibly secret documents for his NKVD controllers.

So the great myth in Russia of the all-seeing and invincible British secret intelligence, which goes back to Britain's attempts to overthrow the early Bolshevik regime after the second 1917 revolution, was, alas, just that – the only spies were those NKVD agents in Britain working faithfully for Moscow.

Towards the end of the war, Blunt was able to develop the ultimate cover story for being a Soviet spy, now not only working for MI5 but also for the royal family, in his capacity as an art historian. As Miranda Carter, his main biographer, has pointed out, his job with them was, in one sense, a dead-end post that no really serious art historian would want to take up, because working for a family as philistine as the British royals was regarded as not really being at the cutting edge of the art world.

(The Courtauld, where Blunt was based for the rest of his academic career, was entirely different – he was to become its director in 1947, aged only forty, and his employment there was the basis of his worldwide scholarly reputation.)

The initial job was cataloguing much of the royal collection, many parts of which were in all kinds of higgledy-piggledy places around the various palaces. Blunt's family had some distant connections with Queen Mary, the widow of King George V (and mother of the then King George VI) and in the tiny world of the court, such links helped. But what helped Blunt the more was the fact that the Surveyor of the King's Pictures, Sir Kenneth Clark (who was also Director of the National Gallery during this time) found the job tiresome, and so gave an opening to Blunt that was to prove invaluable.

For, in 1945, Clark resigned to go on to other things (including, unlike the more academically fastidious Blunt, to try to make art more accessible and popular to a wider audience, such as the famous *Civilization* series on television in the 1960s). Blunt was given the job and, although it was strictly part-time and unpaid, he held it for many decades afterwards, retiring from it not long before he was exposed as a spy, but still holding it *after* his confession of being one in 1964. It was for this, rather than for his connoisseurship or work with the Courtauld that he was knighted by the Queen in 1956, making him Sir Anthony Blunt, and thus in worldly terms by far the most successful of the Cambridge spies. And, as he put it later, who could possibly suspect someone who worked so closely with the royal family as being a Soviet spy? It was the ultimate cover job.

Later on, when exposed in 1979 as a spy, he would strongly aver that he had stopped being a Soviet agent in 1945. This is for many reasons extremely unlikely, as we shall now see.

But there is one series of tasks he undertook for the royal family in Germany after VE day in 1945 that is much loved by conspiracy theorists but in which he might actually be innocent, strange though that might seem.

With the Soviet Red Army well advanced into Germany, there was concern in the British royal family since they had long had very close blood ties with many of the now-deposed royal houses of Germany (who had lost their thrones in 1918 but had retained many of their castles and estates). Blunt was sent with a twofold purpose – one to rescue archives belonging to Queen Victoria, whose eldest daughter Vicky had married Emperor Friedrich of Germany (Kaiser Wilhelm II's father). Then there were many possessions of the House of Hanover still held by the German branch of that dynasty and in danger of capture by the Russians.

Latest thinking on Blunt's adventures in Germany now tend to the opinion that he really was acting in the interests of the royal family after all. The *canard* is that as King George VI's brother and predecessor King Edward VIII, now Duke of Windsor, had been notoriously sympathetic to the Nazis – there was the infamous public handshake with Hitler – that the real and secret purpose of the mission was to scoop up papers of the Windsor's that could embarrass the royal family.

But it seems that the truth is more prosaic. The British wanted to get the Victoria-Vicky correspondence ahead of the Americans, many of whom were cheerfully looting German castles with complete abandon – many articles stolen around this time have now had to be restored to the original owners, to the great embarrassment of their present-day American owners. And while the British royal family shared ancestry with the German-dwelling Kings of Hanover, they had no legal title to any of the heirlooms that they wanted to protect from the Soviets. In fact, some years later, the German branch of the family was able to insist, once the Soviet threat had been removed, to get them back from the United Kingdom. So while Blunt's mission was indeed clandestine, it was nothing that would be of any interest to the NKVD – although while there he did meet Leo Long, one of the Cambridge spies he had recruited himself, and their conversation on their short drive together would indeed have been intriguingly conspiratorial and of great relevance to their Soviet masters.

Once Blunt left MI5 in 1945, he had no direct links to the world of secret intelligence, and to that extent what he said later, in the 1970s when he had been exposed, has some measure of truth to it. A combination of his wartime life and of his very double life as an NKVD agent had clearly taken its toll on his health – his drinking now started to be dangerously high – and colleagues in the art world saw him as retreating increasingly into his shell, not knowing the real reason for his growing introversion and pain. Being a spy was evidently too much of a strain, whether for the British or the Soviets.

But on the other hand, as we now know from the MI5 files and other declassified materials, the idea that he did not work *indirectly* for the NKVD is pure rubbish, certainly up to 1951 and very likely until Philby finally left Britain for Lebanon in 1956.

First, Burgess was giving the NKVD industrial-sized loads of secret documents – as we shall see, especially damaging since he was in the department of the Foreign Office dealing with Korea and he was able to send the USSR extremely confidential details of British and American policy once the Korean war began.

(One of my biggest-ever scoops was, back in the early 1980s, to give the British historian and intelligence specialist Peter Hennessy actual memoranda written by Burgess on the Korean war, proving how important a spy Burgess would have been for the Soviets.)

Much of this was conveyed to Moscow thanks to Blunt's camera – being an art historian he would have the best, and thus Burgess was able to work in tandem with Blunt in giving the NKVD some of the crown jewels of British military thinking and strategy.

Then, as we shall see, in 1951 Burgess and Maclean defected. This was devastating mainly for Kim Philby, but Blunt, a Trinity College and Apostles friend of Burgess, former flatmate in London and fellow homosexual, was naturally under deep suspicion himself.

Liddell, now a very senior MI5 officer, did not want to get a warrant to get into Burgess' flat – so he asked Blunt to do it because he had the key! In retrospect this seems incredible and, during the 1960s and beyond, those who wanted to accuse Liddell of being an NKVD agent himself were to have a field day with this as, once Blunt's treachery was certain, it looked as if there had been a conspiracy between the two men. (In fact, not until 1982 was it finally realised that, however foolish or inept Liddell might have been, he was actually innocent – even if incompetent.)

Blunt's actual hope would have been to cover up the traces and hide all signs of Burgess' spying activities in order to prevent MI5 from discovering who some of his contacts were. As it happens Blunt was either totally inefficient himself – vast swathes of seriously incriminating evidence were left untouched by him – or deliberate, leaving so many possible names of potential traitors that it would deflect attention from him, the real Soviet spy.

And when Goronwy Rees, who had briefly been a Soviet mole, confessed all to the Security Service about Burgess, one of the main problems that Rees had was that, when he was offering information, when he saw Liddell, Blunt was there for lunch as well! Needless to say, this did not help investigations get much further.

Then in 1954, when Kim Philby realised that the net was closing in on him, he used Burgess as a go-between with Yuri Modin, the NKVD (soon-to-be KGB) station officer in London tasked with looking after Moscow's spies. Blunt and Modin met at the Courtauld and they used a postcard to pass on a message to Philby so that Modin and Philby could have a vital and clandestine meeting.

Stuart Hampshire, later a distinguished Oxford academic knighted for services to scholarship, worked with some of the Magnificent Five, including Blunt, in the second world war. (And for this reason was heavily investigated but cleared in 1951 and afterwards.) He suggested to Blunt's biographer, Miranda Carter, that it was possible that Blunt did some kind of confessional deal with MI5 in 1951 and that, as a result, he was let off the hook by the British authorities.

Before the MI5 archives were opened, this idea would have had much credibility, and show how Blunt was able to get away with it. But while plausible and certainly believed by many, it has, like many of the myths, been proved to be untrue. It does not tie in with his help to Modin and Philby in 1954. But we now know the time of the deal – it was thirteen years after Hampshire surmised it happened, in 1964, by accident!

One of Blunt's jobs for the NKVD had been as a talent spotter. One of his recruits was Leo Long, of whom more later, and another was a wealthy young American student at Cambridge, Michael Straight.

By 1963 Straight was highly respectable and the owner of a major American magazine. President Kennedy asked him to become Chairman of the National Endowment for the Arts, and this is where Blunt's past started to unravel. For Straight needed FBI clearance, and as a result he decided to confess his communist past. He had thought of doing so before – he would have saved a lot of grief if he had done so when Burgess was in Washington DC back in 1951 – but now he realised that he had no option. And so he owned up in early 1964 to being a former communist and named Blunt, his recruiter, as an NKVD agent.

After a surprising gap the FBI informed MI5. Blunt's goose was finally cooked and he decided to confess to his treacherous past.

Unfortunately he was able to get an immunity deal, which meant that he never had to pay for his former crimes. He retained both his knighthood and his post at court – one wonders if and when the Queen was ever told that her Surveyor of Pictures was a Soviet spy – and his life continued, for the time being, as normal.

Blunt was, of course, the ultimate establishment insider, and this was a source of profound social resentment to those lower middle class and less privileged members of MI5, some of whom were tasked with interrogating him about his past. One of this group was Peter Wright, an MI5 operative who, like James Jesus Angleton in the CIA, saw spies everywhere and reds under every bed. He and another conspiracy believer, Arthur Martin, tried for eight years to get Blunt to confess more than was actually possible.

(To be fair, an admiralty official without social connections, John Vassall, had been given a long prison term in 1963 for giving secrets to the Soviets after succumbing to blackmail. It could appear like one law for Vassall and another for Blunt – and that is how Martin and Wright would have seen it.)

But however much it might appear that a double standard was being applied, as Christopher Andrew is certainly right to say, the paranoia now unleashed in such circles probably did far more damage to MI5 than anything that Blunt had done during the war. They were convinced that Soviet intelligence had planted dozens of moles in Britain, and they soon included their own boss, Sir Roger

Hollis, the distinguished and, in reality, utterly patriotic and passionately anti-communist director of MI5. For years committees met, investigations took place, the loyalty of countless innocent people was called into question, and turmoil broke out in a way that was entirely damaging to the internal effectiveness of Britain's Security Service. Not even a real mole could have done the damage inflicted by the molehunters, as any reading of *The Defence of the Realm* makes clear.

Not only that, but unlike the time during the Second World War when the NKVD thought of killing Blunt, Burgess and Philby for not unearthing British spies in the USSR, now there really were Russians spying for the British – Oleg Penkovsky, for example, the brave GRU spy whose intelligence for the west was invaluable in preserving world peace during the Cuban missile crisis; Oleg Lyalin, whose defection to the west enabled Britain to expel 105 spies alone in 1971; and above all Oleg Gordievsky who, as we shall see throughout this book was probably the bravest and most successful of all KGB defectors whose intelligence during his time as a British agent gave decades of invaluable material to the west and helped on more than one occasion to prevent the cold war from getting hot.

In other words, far from there being Soviet moles in the west, there were pro-western moles working for the British, the exact opposite of the paranoid beliefs of the molehunters for whom the exposure of Blunt's treachery gave them false and ultimately profoundly damaging beliefs.

For fifteen years after his confession and deal with the British authorities, Blunt was able to continue his art career and academic fame unmolested and untroubled by his past, although the toll on his health was terrible and his drinking increased yet more. He also had to avoid the Queen, though still remained a member of her household until 1972, and he was not given a higher honour on his retirement because the Queen's private secretary, who knew the truth, was able to veto the award.

But many were well aware that he had been a spy and that narrow circle grew ever wider as time progressed. Journalists such as Douglas Sutherland began probes that were all too accurate for Blunt's comfort, and then in 1979 another writer, Andrew Boyle, published a book entitled *The Climate of Treason.* Blunt was not named directly as the Fourth Man but that character was assigned the name 'Maurice' (after an EM Forster book) and it was incredibly obvious to anyone who read the book that Maurice and Blunt were one and the same person.

Would Blunt sue? If he did how would he defend himself? He had prepared himself by retiring as Adviser to the Queen's Pictures, and had published a major work on the significant Italian architect Borromini. For those reasons 1979 should have been an important year for him but now his years as a spy were about to be blown wide open.

Officially, for legal reasons, Boyle did not out Blunt as Maurice though, to an eager audience of Cambridge students listening to him speak not long after the book came out, the connection was obvious. But *Private Eye*, the satirical magazine did so instead.

Margaret Thatcher had not long been Prime Minister by November 1979, and she was no friend of the old, traditional establishment, to whom she would often refer disparagingly as 'the wets'. The Director of MI5, Sir Michael Hanley, would have been appalled at her official naming of Blunt as the Fourth Man, but then she took the advice instead of Sir Michael Havers, the Attorney-General. Thus, when a Labour MP formally asked her if Blunt had indeed been a traitor, she gave the full truth. As she commented about Blunt, it 'damn well serves him right'.

A vast media feeding frenzy then ensued, with various friends of Blunt, both gay and straight, doing all they could to save him from the press mob. His knighthood was taken away, and, much more controversially, he was deprived of his major academic honour, the Fellowship of the British Academy. This created a huge stir, since many eminent scholars felt that he had been elected to it years before for his unique contribution to art history, and that so far as that was concerned, his treachery should make no difference. Some, therefore, such as Oxford historian AJP Taylor resigned their fellowships in protest, while others, such as the leading Cambridge historian Sir Jack Plumb, horrified at the way in which his treason had tarnished the scholarly world, stayed neutral or joined in with his critics. (Technically he resigned in 1980, but after the mood of the majority had become obvious.) Even Trinity College deprived him of his honorary fellowship.

By 1981 he had become exhausted. His partner John Gaskin tried unsuccessfully to commit suicide, but survived, outliving Blunt by five years. His health declined, and on 26th March 1983 he died, revered as an art critic, reviled as a traitor, perhaps in some ways, because of his life outside espionage, the most interesting of all the Cambridge spies.

THE KING OF SPIES
Kim Philby

There is Cambridge, and then there is Trinity College, Cambridge...

Trinity is one of the minority of colleges at both Oxford and Cambridge that are *royal foundations* – colleges founded by a King or Queen. Founded in 1546 by King Henry VIII, the Tudor king who introduced the Reformation to England, it is the merger of two more ancient foundations, King's Hall (of which only a small part now exists) and Michaelhouse. In terms of sheer wealth Trinity exceeds nearly all of the others at Oxford and Cambridge, with an endowment of over £1 billion, and with 32 Nobel Prize winners among its graduates and teaching Fellows. Today, other colleges might be as good academically in terms of degree results (such as Churchill College, founded in honour of Sir Winston Churchill in the 1960s, as a Cambridge equivalent to MIT in the USA), but still no institution even comes near Trinity for sheer prestige, financial clout and the aura of success.

So it is perhaps fitting that four of the five Cambridge spies – Philby, Burgess, Blunt and Cairncross – were all undergraduates at Trinity. (Donald Maclean, the other spy, was at Trinity Hall next door, a much older but smaller and less well-known college). Trinity is famous for its alumni and so its attractions to those who saw themselves as part of a future elite are obvious, in this case the cream of the spies deliberately recruited by the NKVD, the Soviet secret intelligence service later known as the KGB, in order to infiltrate British espionage and society at the very highest levels.

However, there is a very good case for saying that the number one spy, Kim Philby, although definitely part of the British establishment and ruling elite was, in reality, very much an outsider. He had the perfect background and psychology necessary for making him one of the most notorious traitors in the centuries-long history of British espionage.

He was born on New Year's Day 1912, the son of a maverick explorer Harry St John Philby, and his wife Dora. Old Philby was also an outsider and a maverick. He was theoretically an insider: a scholar at Westminster School, the famous school in London which is part of Westminster Abbey, and is known for producing not gentlemen but intellectuals and individualists: Tony Benn and Nick Clegg the politicians and Helena Bonham Carter the actress are currently the best-known Old Westminsters. His son Kim (Harold Adrian Russell, but always called 'Kim') was to follow him both to Westminster and then to Trinity College, Cambridge, with which Westminster School had links.

Philby Senior began conventionally, joining the Indian Civil Service that ran the vast British Raj in India until independence in 1947, but he soon got fed up with conventionality and emigrated to what we now call Saudi Arabia which, at that time, was still a patchwork quilt of warring tribes. These were the days just before the major oil discoveries that transformed the peninsula – until a powerful warlord, Ibn Saud, traditional ruler of the interior state of the Nejd, began a war of conquest that led to the creation of a new country, Saudi Arabia, named after him, in 1932.

St John Philby now stayed most of the time in Saudi Arabia, ostensibly as a businessman but often acting as an explorer and, above all, as Ibn Saud's right-hand man, especially useful to the King in oil negotiations with western powers such as Britain and the USA. So closely did Philby identify with his new surroundings that, in 1930, he converted to Islam and, while he had sometimes been suspected of being a spy for the British, it was clear that his real loyalties lay with Ibn Saud. Indeed, for a short while, he spent time in prison in the United Kingdom for anti-British activities (interestingly at the same time as his son was joining MI6 – SIS or British intelligence).

He returned to the Arabian world where he died in 1960, in Beirut near his now-notorious son rather than in Saudi Arabia, since after Ibn Saud's death in 1953 he had increasingly fallen out of favour with the Saudi regime.

So, like father like son?

Certainly one can say that Kim Philby had what, by any account, could be called a distinctly unusual background. Someone who, despite his establishment Westminster and Trinity College, Cambridge education, was not ever really part of the inner circle of the ruling classes – as he once said, he never betrayed because he never truly belonged.

Similarly, as an atheist from childhood (which would have been very unusual at that time in his social class – Westminster boys had to attend the Abbey every day in term time), he was already marking himself out as apart from the crowd, a loner in a sea of conformists.

One of the key jobs of spies is to tell lies, and here it becomes increasingly hard to elucidate the truth from the myth as the Philby story progresses. Certainly psychologists can make hay with his upbringing but then, as anyone writing about the equally unhappy childhood of, say, Winston Churchill, will attest, two psychologists will probably end up with three theories, at least two of which are mutually contradictory! Guessing can be fun but perhaps fiction might be better than cod psychobabble, and perhaps the best way of understanding Philby is through fiction – through the novels of his friend and fellow-spy Graham Greene and David Cornwell, whose fiction as John le Carré centres closely around the secret world that Philby inhabited. Perhaps the latter's *The Perfect Spy* can tell us more about why someone betrays his country than any work of non-fiction can aspire to achieve.

Either way, by the time that he arrived at Cambridge in late 1929, the safe and secure world of the British Empire, and of the financially stable global economy of the roaring twenties, was about to explode – never again to be restored.

Here we need a short detour, as it is instrumental to the background of all of the Cambridge students who betrayed their country for the Soviet Union back in those troubled times.

The Great Crash of 1929 destroyed economies all over the world. In 1931 in Britain financial crisis turned into political debacle as the Labour (and thus theoretically socialist) government imploded, with the Prime Minister, Ramsay MacDonald. A tiny percentage of his followers joined up with the conservatives and liberals to form what was supposedly a 'national government' to deal with the crisis but it was, in reality, a conservative government in all but name, with MacDonald as a fig-leaf prime minister to disguise conservative power. (And one of the liberal ministers in this coalition was a certain austere Scot, Sir Donald Maclean, of whose son and namesake we shall discover more shortly...)

What was left of the Labour Party was a mere rump of what it had been before and, under its pacifist leader George Lansbury (grandfather of the actress Angela Lansbury), it did not seem to do much politically, either at home or abroad, to fight fascism – the response of much of continental Europe to the disintegration of the west.

Just take the most famous example: the Nazi Party in Germany. In 1928, the year before the crash, they achieved a mere 2.6% of the vote. By 1933 they were Germany's largest single Party and Adolf Hitler was Chancellor, never to lose power in his lifetime. Mussolini had taken over Italy back in the 1920s, and in 1933 Spain began a civil war in which the fascist Falange and militarists around General Franco were to win power, after enormous bloodshed, by

1936. Other regimes in Europe, mainly in the south-east, were to end up with dictatorships of some kind or another in the 1930s, so that the prospects for the democracies were not what one could describe as glowing.

This therefore is the context for the ideological struggles of many concerned young people back at the time when Philby and others were at university. It may all seem fantastic or strange to us now because we have the hindsight of knowing what Hitler's Germany and Stalin's USSR were really like. But this is now and they lived then and, so as with the religious mindset of the Elizabethan period, so too must we attempt to enter the thinking of so many gifted young Cambridge students in a similar time of turmoil, that of the 1930s.

Communism was seen as the enemy of fascism and the democracies were doing next to nothing to actually oppose the Nazis (with honourable exceptions such as Winston Churchill). Or, if they were, they were also opposing rearmament at the same time, which made them look like paper tigers. Only the communists had the 1930s equivalent of street credibility, in terms of being against fascism, in a way that appealed to the young and idealistic.

Many in the 1930s joined the communists, only to repent later. Denis Healey, later to be a Deputy Leader of the Labour Party, was one of them, and when, in August 1939, Nazi Germany and Communist USSR signed a non-aggression pact (sometimes called the Nazi-Soviet Pact or the Molotov-Ribbentrop Pact), countless idealists, such as the Oxford-educated Denis Healey, abjured communism. In Healey's case he joined the more orthodox Labour Party, that believed in both free democracy and in socialism at the same time.

But the big ideological cause during this period was the Spanish civil War, fought between the Falange and the republicans, 1936–1939. As anyone who knows George Orwell's great book *Homage to Catalonia* will recall, in the end this conflict became not a war between oppression and democracy but between two totalitarianisms – that of the extreme right under Franco and of the hard left under the increasingly communist, and thus equally totalitarian, republic. By the time that the fascists won in 1939, democracy had long since lost.

The glamour of the republican cause, though, became global, with volunteers joining up eagerly to fight in the International Brigades; upper-class Oxford and Cambridge-educated Marxist idealists fighting alongside working-class youths from Britain and the USA. One of the former, for instance, was Esmond Romilly, Jessica Mitford's first husband and nephew by marriage of Winston Churchill.

We should not be surprised, therefore, that many Cambridge students from well-bred families supported communism during this period. What is different about those who later betrayed their country to spy for the USSR was that *they continued to be communists*, especially after August 1939, when the sheer cynicism of the Nazi-Soviet Pact jolted people out of their idealism – after all, how could one support an ideology that deemed it all right to do a deal with Hitler?

The other thing to notice is that, in the same way that the USA and capitalism are synonymous today, so too, for most of its existence down to 1991, was the USSR seen as the bulwark of communism – what was in the interests of the Soviet Union was the same as those of the communist ideology it purported to represent. To be a communist was thus to support the USSR, since if the USSR went, so too would communism and the global ideology that it enabled. Come August 1939 this was to be the 'get out of jail card' for continuing communists like Kim Philby and his fellow spies – to ally with a state like Nazi Germany seemed strange, even treacherous. But if the USSR needed to do so to survive, to let the capitalist or reactionary countries in the west fight each other, then communism in the USSR would survive and thus globally as an ideology as well.

As we now know, Stalin's error in 1939 did not prevent Nazi Germany invading the USSR in 1941, with over 20 million Soviet citizens dying during the rest of the Second World War. But this is with hindsight – Marxism and the inevitable victory of communism seemed, like a religious belief, to be so sure to its adherents that faith in Stalin, for the young Cambridge spies, was as great as that of their sixteenth-century predecessors in the Pope and the inevitability of the Catholic reconversion of England.

Oleg Kalugin, a senior KGB official who in the 1970s helped to look after Kim Philby in Moscow – improving his living facilities, seeing that he was cared for, and used by the KGB for advice and avuncular wisdom – has made an interesting point in his memoirs *Spy Master*. It is an interesting one that those who have heard current Russian successor spymasters also make when speaking off the record in the west. In the 1930s the Soviet cause, while linked to the security of the USSR, was primarily *ideological*. Philby always told Kalugin that he never spied for the money, and that is probably true – he did so for *communism*, for his *beliefs*.

But for what does the present Russian Federation recruit its own spies? Those we have discovered, such as Aldrich Ames in the USA, seem to have been entirely financial in motive – sheer greed in other words. People are betraying their country *for money* and not for anything in which they *believe*. Russia no longer stands for anything in the way that the USSR once did when it embodied Marxist-Leninism. This is a major change – people spying for money could in theory spy for anyone, since if greed is their motive, then profit could come from any source. The days of Cold War espionage – the west standing for freedom and the east for communism are now well and truly over: it seems that even China is primarily non-ideological in the way in which it recruits spies, especially those with whom it has no obvious ethnic ties.

In a sense, therefore, Philby and the others in the Magnificent Five (Blunt, Maclean, Burgess and Cairncross) were *among* the last of a kind, and certainly the most eminent: the 'Romeo spies' of the later Cold War. Especially handsome Stasi (East German) agents who seduced lonely and plain spinsters working for NATO were recruiting on a very different basis to the ones for which Philby and his friends were determined to devote their lives.

And one thing to note in passing – the majority of the Cambridge spies were confirmed *heterosexuals*. Because Burgess and Blunt were, as we shall see, firmly the other way and part, therefore, of a 1930s gay underground as much as the conspiratorial world of Soviet agents, sex was not the prime *motif* in our story, although it might well have been in the case of these two individuals. As for Philby, he was a womaniser all his life; multiply married and, apart from his first marriage of convenience, someone who did so for love. That is, of course, to reuse a phrase of another famous Trinity graduate, if he knew 'whatever love means...'.

Let us therefore revert to our story.

Philby himself was not recruited while an undergraduate in Cambridge: the idea that he was so enlisted is actually a myth – and the problem of writing about spies is that they create all kinds of myths about themselves as part of their tradecraft and legend. He did, however, become a communist while an undergraduate at Trinity, especially after what many regarded as the political treachery of James Ramsay MacDonald in 1931 in abandoning a minority Labour government to form a 'national government' with the conservatives. He initially read history, where he was not so academically successful, before switching to economics, where he came under the influence of the eminent – and very overtly Marxist – economist, Maurice Dobb, whose left-wing reading group he eagerly joined.

Philby was a member of the University Socialist Society but never, unlike Dobb, a communist in public gaze. However, even if he had been, it is only in retrospect that such links would have been regarded as suspicious because of his later treachery. At the time many a *bien pensant* undergraduate had left-wing if not ostensibly communist views, and it was regarded by the older generation as a rite of passage, and certainly nothing to frighten the horses, provided of course that people grew out of such nonsense and acquired the wisdom of their elders.

But for Philby, his conversion to communism was the real thing. Having become an atheist as a child, he now had his new religion, one that he was to hold onto tenaciously for the rest of his life.

His background suggested various public careers, including the Indian Civil Service (which, despite its name, was in effect filled with white people who ran the British Raj) and the Foreign Office. His attempts to get into these ran into difficulties, his left-wing views being only part of the problem. But in order to improve his German, just in case the Foreign Office did want him – for which he would have to pass a stiff exam – he went to Vienna, and there began what was to turn out to be his *real* lifelong career.

1930s Vienna was at the heart of the ideological struggle then raging in Europe. In 1933 Engelbert Dollfuss had taken dictatorial powers in Austria, setting up a non-Nazi but clearly fascist regime. His main domestic opposition were the communists, based in the districts in the capital known as Red Vienna, and the local Nazis (we must not forget that Hitler was born in Austria) were also not inactive. Philby, working for a communist front organisation, was thus entering one of the tinderboxes of Europe. Italian fascist dictator Mussolini was also taking an interest in Austria since, at that time, he still feared German encroachment through Austria in case the new Third Reich wished to reclaim territory that the victorious Allies had taken from the defunct Austrian Empire and given to Italy after the war. A lot was at stake in Vienna and an effective civil war was raging, and Philby was right there in the middle of it.

Here he was well in with the communist resistance. One of those he met was 'Litzi', or Alice Friedman, and this meeting was to change his life. As the fighting grew worse – and more disadvantageous to the communists, who were bombarded into submission – he decided to get Litzi out to safety. In those days marriage conferred instant British citizenship and, by marrying Litzi, he was thus able to easily help her to sanctuary in England. This was, basically, a briefly-consummated marriage of convenience, which lasted legally until he was already a member of the Secret Intelligence Service (MI6) after the war, when he married his mistress and the mother of his children, Aileen Furse, in December 1946. But he soon had lovers and some may even have been genuine, though in the case of a dissembler like Philby it is impossible to know.

But the main difference Litzi made was that she knew of communists in England. One of these was a lady named Edith Tudor-Hart, an Austrian Jewess, like Litzi herself, and married to a British doctor and fellow communist Alex Tudor-Hart. She, in turn, knew some real Soviet spies, and so it was through his link with her that he was finally contacted by the NKVD and his career as a traitor began. His trip to Vienna had made a difference he could not have imagined.

So Kim Philby, the key member of the Cambridge spy ring, the Five, was actually recruited not in some ancient Cambridge court (the University term for what we would normally call a quadrangle, or quad at rival Oxford) but rather more prosaically on a park bench in Regent's Park in London, on 1st June 1934.

In his memoirs Philby refers to someone he codenamed 'Otto'. He guesses that Otto might be Austrian – and then maybe Czech. In fact we know the man's real name: a rather unusual NKVD officer called Arnold Deutsch, who was in fact Austrian, and was involved in the 'sex-pol' movement (sic!) back in Vienna – a seriously flaky sexual cult that believed that bad orgasm repressed the proletariat and increased the domination of the capitalist classes. (In other words, a sect so weird that you could not possibly make it up...) Needless to say, this kind of sexual/political anarchism did not go down too well with the Austrian police, and Deutsch and his family were obliged to flee, coming to England in time to recruit Philby to the NKVD.

Philby had scared Edith Tudor-Hart by saying that he wanted to be an active communist, and Otto/Deutsch confirmed her view – if you wanted to be a spy for the NKVD, then it was best to give the Communist Party as wide a berth as possible. Agents should perfect an alternative personality in which no communist links or beliefs of any kind would ever be suspected. They would thus have a story that would convince the British establishment that you were one of their own, a good chap who could be admitted to the inner sanctum without any further ado. Or as Deutsch told his impressionable new young charge, someone known to be an overt communist 'would never get near the real truth' but 'someone moving as a real bourgeois among the bourgeois could'.

Deutsch and the NKVD were not to know that a background as unusual as Philby's was hardly normal bourgeois – that spy was to be Maclean *par excellence* – but he was as good as they could get for now.

Deutsch also seems to have become a father-like figure to young Kim, though there was not such a large age gap between them. Once again psychologists could have a field day, with Deutsch as the paternal substitute for the erratic St John, but whatever the truth, the working relationship got off to an excellent start.

Deutsch was recalled to the USSR during Stalin's purges but unlike some of Philby and the Magnificent Five's other Soviet controllers, he was not shot for treason by the paranoid NKVD. His fate is uncertain but he might have died on active service in 1942, unlike his immediate successor in London, Theodore Maly, who was shot as a supposed German spy. Being Philby's link with Moscow could be a dangerous business...

Much of what we know – or think we know – about Philby is from his own memoirs *My Secret War*. But as the British historian EDR Harrison has argued, in a book on intelligence and diplomacy, as has Robert Cecil, a fellow member of MI6 (and in his case a patriot), relying on the memoirs of a spy, someone trained to lie twice over, first *for* his own country and then *to* his own country as being a spy for another power, is a seriously unreliable thing to do. Philby lied about his own loyalties for nearly thirty years and, when he wrote his memoirs, it was in Moscow, under the auspices of his bosses in the NKVD, who intended his book to be as harmful as possible to the west.

As Harrison puts it: '*My Silent War* is a striking example of KGB propaganda... as a political weapon.' And now that some of the KGB archive has been opened, as well as the official histories of MI5 and MI6 written in Britain, we can get a good idea of how much of what he writes is even true.

Much of it, as Christopher Andrew, the official historian of MI5 has shown, is pure lies, designed to humiliate Britain and the USA, and build up a myth of an all-powerful and invincible KGB.

And as Robert Cecil recalls, while Philby was unquestionably very important, and would have become unbelievably so if he had ever risen to the top of MI6, one could also argue that the atomic bomb spies – Alan Nunn May and Klaus Fuchs from the British side and those like the Krogers on the American – who betrayed the secrets of the atomic bomb to the USSR were also of very considerable importance themselves.

So, with everything on Philby, it is a case of *caveat emptor* – or in our case, let the reader beware! There is no doubt that Philby was a major traitor, sending countless agents to their deaths (and, as Oleg Kalugin noticed when chatting to him in later years, clearly without any remorse). But there is also a lot of mythology surrounding the Philby case, and he would naturally wish to exaggerate his own importance in order to increase the embarrassment of the west. And this too we should not forget.

Philby was able to recruit some of his fellow Cambridge communists as spies – why Oxford has no famous spies remains a mystery: either they were too clever ever to be caught or, because the NKVD had success with Cambridge, they did not bother so much with Oxford. Or perhaps Oxford, unlike Cambridge, was too patriotic to spy for the enemy – it was certainly not for lack of communist undergraduates at the older university. (And probably, alas, we might never know the answer...)

But over the course of the next few years the recent graduates of Cambridge University became the group we know by their Soviet nickname, the 'Magnificent Five': Kim Philby, Anthony Blunt, Donald Maclean, Guy Burgess and John Cairncross, the last of whom managed to avoid detection for decades and to avoid prosecution even when discovered, and is also the least known. There were others: Leo Long and an American, Michael Straight, and a scientist, Alan Nunn May. (In fact there could have been more but, as with the Oxford spies, it is now impossible to know...) But it is the 'Five' who have become infamous, and the next chapters will give more details of their careers as traitors and spies for Moscow.

One of Deutsch's key requirements of his spies was for them to sever and disguise all links to the Communist Party. In the case of both Burgess and Philby, they were to join far-right groups, which had the precise opposite views on the major threats to Britain in the 1930s than that of the USSR and the Communist Party. The Anglo-German Fellowship, which Philby joined, and which had many establishment pro-appeasement if not actually pro-Nazi figures in its membership, was thus the last place in which anyone would normally look for a Soviet spy.

In those days people saw the London *Times* newspaper as the pillar of the establishment. And while it was Donald Maclean who first managed to get inside the Foreign Office and the corridors of power (as we shall see), for Kim Philby to get a job as a reporter in February 1937 in Spain, to cover the Spanish civil war after it broke out in 1936, was a major coup both for him and for his Soviet controllers. And he was careful to cultivate the image of someone pro-Franco, the falangist/nationalist leader, and avoid links with the International Brigades, the brave but often foolhardy sympathisers with the republican regime. As many fighters in the Brigades were overt communists (including Josip Broz, later known as Tito, the long-time ruler of the former Yugoslavia), this was rather ironic, and again provided Philby with the perfect cover he needed to disguise his true sympathies.

In August 1939 Hitler and Stalin agreed a non-aggression Pact – called, as we saw, the Nazi-Soviet Pact. They agreed to be friendly neutrals to each other, and, still worse, to carve up Poland between them, along with other parts of central Europe. (This is a betrayal that is still actively remembered with much distaste by generations of Poles, especially as they never regained the territory they lost to Stalin and then had to suffer over 40 years of communist rule.) Decent socialists, such as the future British political leader Denis Healey, were horrified and many abandoned their communism because of Stalin's deal with the ultimate fascist enemy, Nazi Germany. What was the point of being in a 'popular front' of communists, socialists and others against fascism when the main communist country betrayed everything by signing a peace pact *with Hitler*? But while many, like Healey, made the right conclusion, abandoned communism and joined the armed forces the better to fight Nazism, others, like Philby, clearly had different views. Because his memoirs were written under KGB supervision, it is hard to know exactly what the young Philby felt about this event – which enabled Hitler only to have to fight on one front, against France and the west. Maybe he briefly faltered in his loyalty... But either way it made no real difference.

When the Second World War broke out in 1939 the British establishment, which had hitherto recruited mainly through merit-based exams to its Civil Service and Diplomatic Service, needed to recruit far more people than was usually necessary. Thousands of people had to be signed up for active government work or special military operations purely through friendship and acquaintance, and so all the usual checks and safeguards went by the board. (And even with them Maclean had still entered the Foreign Office, to rise swiftly in its ranks – counter-espionage was still at its infancy at this time and was virtually non-existent.)

So, after just a few months as a journalist covering the war, Philby found himself in what was to become the Special Operations Executive, SOE, then called Section D of the Secret Intelligence Service, SIS – but known to everyone then and since as MI6.

(In wartime several other MI organisations existed – MI9, for example, helped prisoners of war to escape from Germany. But it is MI6 that spied overseas, and MI5 the Security Service, which ran security at home, that survived and became famous.)

If he had stayed there Philby would soon have been dispatched to blow up bridges abroad. Many SOE operatives were communists, and many of the locals with whom they worked to fight the German occupation were as well. In Yugoslavia, for example, British and American sympathisers with communism in the SOE and its US equivalent OSS, were able to persuade Churchill to back the communist guerrillas under Tito fighting axis forces there. In this case with strong military justification, since Tito's communist partisans were, as Churchill realised and told others, killing far more Germans than the other resistance groups. Of course, most SOE operatives, including the writer Evelyn Waugh and Churchill's own son Randolph, were as far from communist as one could imagine. But it is interesting that, had Philby stayed in SOE, he would have been far from alone in his political allegiance.

In 1941 Hitler invaded the USSR, to the horror of Stalin who had disregarded the warnings from both Britain and from his own spies that this would happen. Philby was now at least on the same side of the war as his spymasters, as the Soviet Union and United Kingdom became allies, with the USA joining in after Pearl Harbor in December that year.

By this time Philby's time in Spain had paid dividends. He joined the Iberian section of MI6, and was thus ushered into the very organisation dreamed of for him by his Soviet controllers – with whom he was now back in touch. And here is a wonderful irony... The NKVD, as paranoid as ever, could hardly believe its luck in getting such key recruits. So much so that, for a while, they wondered if the Magnificent Five and their other agents (British and American) were really *double agents,* ostensibly working for Moscow but actually working for the British all along and only pretending to be Soviet spies. This was, in fact, not the case but it is interesting nonetheless to observe that the NKVD nearly threw away their own jewels in the crown!

How much damage Philby did during the war – until 1944 – is hard to gauge as some books have an interest in exaggerating his potency while others wish to downplay it.

He was certainly doing Britain no good, but whether he had quite the role that the popular books on Cambridge spies attribute to him is difficult to assess, since so much of what he did (rather ironically) remains secret! Secret that is to historians – the USSR would have known exactly what he gave them, though as specialists have pointed out, whether or not they *understood* the significance of the vast amounts of material that he and the others in the Magnificent Five were providing for them is open to question. As both British and Russian experts have suggested, the NKVD was very good at collecting information but often terrible at processing it. Paranoid rulers from Stalin to Andropov often had their own view of reality and the truth provided by spies was thus often ignored or disbelieved. And, as we shall see, during the war itself spies such as John Cairncross often had far more valuable information than Philby, even if the latter was a rising star in the intelligence world.

And for Philby it now got even better... and thus also for his masters in Moscow.

Churchill had long since realised that, while the USSR was an ally against Hitler, long term it was unlikely that the west and the Soviets would remain friends – as indeed presciently turned out to be the case. So MI6 set up Section 9, whose main task it was 'to collect and interpret information concerning communist espionage and subversion'. *And in 1944 the head of this section was Kim Philby, a communist agent of the USSR.*

In other words, the fox had been put in charge of the henhouse! The Soviets could not possibly have dreamed of having a better spy in a better place! (Which, incidentally, by the 1950s, they began to suspect as being *truly* too good to be true – once again he was suspected of being a double agent.) The person in charge of finding Soviet agents was one himself! Philby had ruthlessly manoeuvred himself into this position, getting rid of genuine patriots like his colleague Felix Cowgill, for example, and was now in a position to do the maximum damage possible.

Of course he had to be careful – too many blunders, too many sabotaged missions, and he would either have been sacked for inefficiency or revealed as a Soviet mole. (Anyone who reads *Tinker, Tailor, Soldier, Spy* will get a wonderful impression of how Philby must have operated in reality as the Bill Haydn character does in the novel.) But if he had too many successes for MI6 he would be damaging his spymasters, the NKVD (or NKGB and later KGB as the organisation became). It cannot have been an easy balance for him to strike.

And it soon almost came to a premature end! Two Soviet intelligence officers decided in August/September 1945 to defect to the west. Both of them could have had information to unmask Philby as a spy. But as *he* was the person in charge of finding Soviet spies, he was able in the first case to downgrade the threat and in the second to eliminate it altogether.

In the first instance, Igor Gouzenko and his family defected to the Canadians. This was fortunate since the defection had already happened by the time that Philby knew of it. But in this case he was able to prevent the real expert, a lady called Jane Archer, from being the interrogator. While Gouzenko certainly had information that showed that there were spies for the USSR working in western intelligence – including in Canada and the USA –

Philby was able to narrowly avoid any suspicions focussing on *him*.

With the other defector, Konstantin Volkov, Philby was, astonishingly, able to remove the threat altogether. As Volkov defected through Istanbul, and wanted money for his information, Philby was able to postpone Volkov's actual escape, warn the NKGB in Moscow that Volkov was a traitor, and so allow the Soviets to send two thugs to Istanbul to kidnap Volkov and bring him back to the USSR, where he was shot. Volkov could easily have unmasked Philby and, as it turns out, a further 313 other Soviet agents as well. The effect of Volkov's successful defection would have been catastrophic for the USSR but, as it was, it was Volkov who was shot and Philby who emerged unscathed, giving him what he later called 'a very narrow squeak indeed'.

(Other things were happening at this time with the Magnificent Five, along with Cambridge spies Alan Nunn May, who confessed to espionage, and Leo Long. But to avoid complicating this chapter we shall deal with them later on. Suffice it to say here that Philby's behaviour *should* have alerted the British, Canadian and US authorities to the fact that something strange was going on – but it was not until 1951, when Burgess and Maclean defected to Moscow, the former we now know by mistake, that Philby was himself suspected.)

Philby also now finally got married to Aileen, the mother of his children. The fact that he took so long, and that he had spent the war legally married to Litzi, was something that, fortunately for him, the intelligence services, both MI5 and MI6, had overlooked.

In 1946 he was posted to Turkey, a major Cold War listening spot as we would now call it, and he was even given an honour by the government, an OBE. Indeed, so well was he doing that he was even beginning to be thought of as a future head of MI6, or 'C' to use the correct initial. ('M' is Ian Fleming's imaginary name for the post – 'C' comes from Cumming, the first letter of the surname of the founding director.)

Then in 1949 his luck improved dramatically again – he was made the MI6 liaison in Washington DC with the USA, including therefore with the newly created CIA, the eventual successor organisation of the wartime Office of Strategic Services (OSS). (Truman abolished the OSS, then re-established the CIA after an interval. Like the OSS, the CIA is involved in both espionage and special operations which, in Britain, were separated during the war with MI6 looking after intelligence while the Special Operations Executive handled sabotage.)

And here Philby was given access to one of the biggest and most successful secrets of the cold war!

This was the VENONA secret – the fact that, for a brief moment in 1945, the west (principally the National Security Agency in the US) had been able to decrypt Soviet diplomatic and intelligence messages. It was not that simple – the spies all had code names (Philby was STANLEY by this time) and names and codenames and circumstances had to be matched. But as we shall see, the VENONA decrypts – at which the USA continued to work for decades – had been able to unmask the atom bomb spies, such as Klaus Fuchs and Alan Nunn May and, by the time that Philby got to Washington DC, they were close to getting

HOMER, alias of the now leading British diplomat Donald Maclean.

By a nice irony, *so* secret for a while was VENONA that not even the president of the USA himself was able to know of its existence. But Kim Philby *did* know, and he was a Soviet spy! And this of course meant, therefore, that the NKGB (soon to be KGB) also knew of the secret – because he told them! And for the two years he was in Washington DC they were able to know what he knew, even if the President of the USA did not.

Philby was also highly thought of by many in the CIA, including, fatefully as things would evolve, by James Jesus Angleton, one of the swiftly up-and-coming CIA analysts and a future major power in that organisation. Only the FBI harboured suspicions that all was not as it should be with their British ally.

Then, in 1950, the wheels very slowly began to come unstuck, and not in a way that he could have expected. Guy Burgess was posted to Washington DC in 1950 and, as we shall see later in this book, he was notoriously badly behaved and completely indiscreet about his homosexuality in a day in which such proclivities were firmly illegal. Philby made the mistake of thinking it best if Burgess stayed at the Philby household – where he could keep an eye on his wayward fellow spy – not realising that this drew close attention to his long-lasting links with Burgess.

By 1951 the authorities finally realised that HOMER was Maclean. This, in and of itself, put Philby in acute danger since he was worried about what would happen were the now distinctly fragile Maclean to succumb to aggressive interrogation. And here Philby's plans were now unravelling. He had preferred to use Burgess as a cut-out between himself and his Soviet controllers, through a Soviet illegal named HARRY based in New York. (As always, things in Moscow were uncertain and chaotic, as Philby clearly realised: the myth of the all-omnipotent KGB once again proving itself to be false.) However, now Burgess behaved himself so badly that he had to be sent home to Britain, so drunken and dishevelled that he was under no suspicion himself.

Once back in London, Burgess and Maclean were often spotted together. Philby was worried that Maclean would spill the beans so asked Moscow to rescue Maclean and take him to the USSR – *but not in collaboration with Burgess.* Unfortunately for Philby, it was just this that happened. It seems that Plan A was for Burgess to take Maclean to Moscow and then come home to see if he could pick up the wreckage of his own Foreign Office career (or indeed any job at all). But once Burgess and Maclean successfully fled to Moscow in 1951 (of which more in another chapter) the Soviets insisted that Burgess stay. It seemed that they felt they had two burned-out cases so they might as well keep both of them under wraps in Russia.

So now it became the flight of the *two* spies: Burgess and Maclean. While Maclean had been correctly suspected it seems that Burgess had not been, though how he had managed to evade suspicion seems, in retrospect, truly extraordinary.

And the flight of *Burgess*, who had until weeks before been Philby's lodger in Washington DC, raised all kinds of suspicions now against Philby himself, and with terrible timing, since Philby had only just begun talks not only to continue as MI6 liaison officer in DC but of MI5 as well – in which case he really would have given the crown jewels to his Moscow masters.

Now suddenly *he* was under suspicion – the often spoken-of future head of MI6!

Some in MI5 had suspected him, as had others in the FBI (the CIA seems to have been shocked, especially Angleton, with disastrous results that we shall see later on). Philby was now summoned home, and interrogated by 'Buster' Milmo, a leading barrister, and by Jim Skardon, the top interrogator who had been so effective in breaking down Klaus Fuchs.

Philby was made of sterner stuff, however, and did not crack. And first, the British decided that they could not use the VENONA decrypts in court evidence, even though, as some in both MI5 and MI6 realised, the secret was out since, if Philby was indeed now a proven Soviet agent, his controllers in Moscow would know all about VENONA as well. And second, British interrogators played by Queensberry rules, in effect trying for a confession, and this, in 1951, Philby refused to give them.

So he was now out of the service, but with many of those still in it unable to believe that their golden boy really was a traitor: he had played his cards so well that he still managed to have supporters despite the suspicions of others and the growing evidence that his links to Burgess and Maclean proved his treachery.

(We shall look at the fallout of the defection in relation to Blunt and Cairncross in another chapter – both of them had very close shaves in 1951.)

In 1955 things even came to Philby's advantage, by mistake. A Labour MP with a strong sense of how things were going asked the Foreign Secretary, Harold Macmillan, if it were true that Kim Philby was the 'Third Man', a spy like Burgess and Maclean. (The title came from Graham Greene's novel of post-war Vienna – although Greene had been in MI6 along with Philby, the book considerably predates the accusation.)

Of course Philby was guilty. And indeed the VENONA decrypts now pointed to him conclusively – but, as Christopher Andrew shows in his definitive and official book on MI5 history, the internal communication system was not working properly and so Macmillan had no option but to proclaim Philby's innocence, under British rules of evidence, in which one is innocent until proven guilty.

Philby had, since 1951, been obliged to maintain a low cover, frequently getting drunk and being terrible to his wife Aileen (who died in 1957 of multiple illnesses, almost certainly exacerbated by knowledge of her husband's guilt). In 1954, through Anthony Blunt, he had been in touch with the Soviet link at their embassy, Yuri Modin (whose book *My Five Cambridge Friends* is a fascinating read, albeit written from a very different angle than Christopher Andrew's wonderful *The Defence of the Realm* and *The Mitrokhin Archive,* the latter two being of invaluable help for this and many other chapters of this book). But the years of degeneracy were now transformed by his official clearance. He was now made Middle East correspondent of *The Observer,* being posted to Beirut in 1956, and with many of his links with MI6 rekindled by those who still believed in him.

Here he flourished, and got remarried to Eleanor Brewer, the ex-wife of an American journalist. All seemed to be going well for him – though we will not know how much in touch he still was with MI6 for some time as those archives remain hermetically sealed (again surely ironically since if the Soviets knew what he was telling them, we should now be able to know too!).

But in 1961 another defector, Anatoly Golitsyn, came over to the west, and he was able to fill in a very considerable number of pieces in the jigsaw for MI5 as well as for the Americans. Those who did not believe in Philby felt that they now had the information that they needed to prove his guilt.

Once again, though, the British establishment played by Queensberry rules. In 1963 the intelligence services thought it best if Philby simply confessed, in return for a deal of immunity (of the kind that Blunt made in 1964, as we will soon discover). And they sent over an MI6 friend of his Nicholas Elliott, to persuade him to confess.

Philby, as Christopher Andrew reminds us, was ever the accomplished liar. He gave the impression to Elliott that he had not really been a spy after 1946, which of course was sheer nonsense, as 1946 to 1951 had been his best and most effective years for Moscow. Elliott unfortunately believed it.

But Philby now realised that he had, in fact, confessed something – and since he always perpetuated the lie that one *never* confesses he decided that the time had come to jump ship, in his case literally. When Elliott went back to hear more, he found that the bird had flown the coop and that Philby had vanished, as we now know to Moscow. He really had been the Third Man but had only proved it by defecting to the USSR.

There has been huge speculation about Philby ever since; some to the effect that he really was a double after all and that MI6 was letting him go knowingly to Moscow in order to stir things up there. Subsequent KGB defectors and authorised histories of MI6 and MI5 have shown that however attractive this idea might be – that Philby *really was ours after all* – it is alas all nonsense, and that he truly was what he said: a Soviet spy in the west for nearly three decades.

Arrival in Moscow was a major shock for him. He was treated shabbily. Not for nearly ten years until Yuri Andropov headed the KGB and asked Oleg Kalugin to look after Philby was he given the comforts and status that his decades of loyalty to Moscow should surely have warranted. When he told people he held high rank in the KGB, this was all lies – only native citizens could do this – and for many years, during which time he ended his marriage to Eleanor and had an affair with Donald Maclean's wife Melinda, he lived in growing squalor and neglect.

Although his treachery had been long suspected by some, it certainly did not help Anglo-American relations. No one was more hurt than James Jesus Angleton, now in charge of counter-intelligence in the CIA. No theory was too paranoid to be believed, and spies were swiftly seen everywhere where in reality none existed.

And so one could say that some of Philby's best work for the KGB was in fact accomplished after he arrived in Moscow.

This was not the publication of his memoir *My Silent War,* his supposed (though apparently genuinely written) autobiography, which was designed to perpetuate the myth of an all-powerful, highly successful KGB. Intelligence experts have called the book 'entirely bogus' however, being 'highly selective' and designed 'to spill his former employer's beans...'. Just one example – he was never an actual KGB officer, just one of their agents. Admittedly he was perhaps one of their best ever in this category, but even for Philby the KGB did not change its rules – as we have seen, his first decade or so in Moscow was totally squalid, and it took well into the 1970s for his employers even to make good use of his knowledge, services and insights into western life.

Rather, I would suggest, it was the paranoia that Philby's defection in 1963 aroused in certain sections of the CIA and MI5 that his real and long-term damage was done. James Jesus Angleton can be argued never to have recovered from his erstwhile friend and colleague Kim Philby's treachery. As a result, Angleton spent decades of the rest of his own life looking for spies in the CIA that simply did not exist. There *were* KGB (and later SVR, Russian Federation overseas secret intelligence) spies working for Moscow, but much later on, such as Aldrich Ames, who was a spy in the 1980s and 1990s (Angleton retired from the CIA in 1975). During Angleton's time in real power in counter-intelligence, all sorts of innocent people were accused of being Soviet agents (or 'moles', the term popularised in the brilliant John le Carré novels) and no one could trust anyone for a long while. An actual KGB agent could not have done a better job of creating inward turmoil within the

CIA than Angleton's 'molehunts' that took place in the decade following Philby's defection to Moscow.

And this applied to the United Kingdom and to MI5 and MI6 as well. By 1964 Blunt had confessed, as we shall see, and agreed an immunity deal with the British authorities. Cairncross, the final member of the Magnificent Five, did not quite do the same but managed to stay abroad, his espionage days over. Various genuine but minor spies and 'agents of influence' were unearthed in the 1960s, including, for example, a Labour MP, Bernard Floud, who committed suicide in 1967 when discovered.

But there was no major Soviet spy in either MI5 or MI6 waiting to be revealed! Not that this convinced Angleton's equivalents in Britain, the most notorious being Peter Wright, of MI5. He had links with Lord Rothschild, who had been a brave MI5 operative during the war, but whose educational overlap at Cambridge with the Magnificent Five caused him endless heartache. Wright was also close to various journalists, who loved the idea of getting into exposés and dark secrets.

All this was, as in the US case, pure paranoia. But molehunts and committees spawned and existed for years, with the names and careers of totally innocent people being dragged through the mud. Most infamous of these was that of Sir Roger Hollis, who became head of MI5. Endless investigations proved this, including one by Sir Burke Trend, the revered secretary to the cabinet and guardian of Britain's greatest secrets for many years. Trend found Hollis innocent, as did all the other probes into the past.

Some of this was confusion. Those of a paranoid tendency were sure that the person known in VENONA as

ELLI *must* be Hollis. In fact this was rubbish – ELLI was indeed a genuine Soviet agent, but in fact Leo Long, a Cambridge contemporary of the 'Five'.

But surely part of it was the belief in the great Soviet lie, the supposed brilliance and effectiveness of the KGB (and its military equivalent, the GRU). There *had* to be more spies, surely? And so, for decades, the hunts for secret traitors (nicknamed "moles" by some, thus called molehunts) continued and in time got out into the public: books with which Wright was active in helping, such as Chapman Pincher's *Their Trade is Treachery* and Wright's own notorious autobiography, *Spycatcher*, which the British government in the 1980s foolishly publicised by trying to get it banned in the Australian courts.

However, all this was complete nonsense, as were attempts to find fourth and fifth men other than those who really were guilty (as we shall soon see, the fourth being Anthony Blunt and the fifth John Cairncross).

And how do we know this? The answer is in fact quite simple. The one thing that intelligence agencies cannot do is to publicise their triumphs! The British could hardly have announced during the Second World War that they had broken the Enigma codes and could read German SIGINT (signals intelligence). Nor could the NKVD have trumpeted Philby's treachery, say, in 1949. So for many years British intelligence had to keep secret *how* they knew who really had been traitors and who was innocent.

For the answer is that they had two amazing spies. One, Oleg Gordievsky, was one of the most successful MI6 agents of all time, rising high in the ranks of the KGB. And, for example, when Mikhail Gorbachev was about to come to power, and visited Britain, Gordievsky, as the key KGB man in London wrote the briefing on Thatcher for Gorbachev; then, as a spy for MI6, wrote a similar briefing in reverse, on Gorbachev for Mrs Thatcher. And as a senior member of the KGB he knew exactly who was a spy and who was not, that the Magnificent Five were indeed Soviet agents, but that Sir Roger Hollis, by contrast, was totally innocent. But until Gordievsky had to flee to the west (undoubtedly betrayed by the treachery of Aldrich Ames in the USA), the huge British/MI6 coup in having him as an agent in place for so long had to be one of the world's most closely guarded secrets.

More remarkable in some ways was Vasili Mitrokhin, a KGB operative and later on senior archivist, who managed to smuggle out the names of hundreds of Soviet agents in the west in shoeboxes! He too was able to show exactly who was whom, and give more detail (used in writing this chapter, from the book he wrote with Christopher Andrew) on what Philby and the others were up to during their time as NKVD spies in the west.

So Philby was guilty, and Hollis innocent – and now we can all know why we know!

As we have seen, Philby's last years in Moscow improved after the decade or so of alcoholic stupor and neglect. In 1970 he met and, in 1971 married, Rufina Ivanova, a part-Russian, part-Polish chemistry and furs expert. This time he found final happiness – or maybe he was just too old for his previous promiscuous ways. With Andropov and Kalugin improving his living standards and utilising his expertise, he was also able to travel, though naturally only to safely pro-Soviet countries, such as Cuba.

He was able to meet up with curious British journalists, the best known being the investigative reporter Phillip Knightley, who interviewed him at length and published widely-read articles and books as a result of their meetings. (But, in fact, the best Knightley book to read is his much later *A Hack's Progress*, with a chapter on Philby, in which Knightley is able to make use of material that we now know was unknown to him at the time of his meetings with Philby in Moscow and during the earlier-still *Sunday Times* exposés of the Cambridge spy ring.)

And in 1988 Philby died on 11th May, given, at last, a hero's burial by a now finally grateful KGB. But just over three years later, the Soviet Union, which he had served so loyally for over half a century, was no more. And so too was the era of ideological spies. Russia is no communist state, whatever else it might be. Spies, even towards the end of the Soviet era, like Ames, did it for the money, and now no one in the west would surely risk all to defend the national interests of Russia *as Russia*. Philby, therefore, almost certainly died the last of his kind.

THE CASE OF THE MISSING DIPLOMATS

Guy Burgess & Donald Maclean

Marks and Spencer, Procter and Gamble, Laurel and Hardy, Morecombe and Wise – some names seem always to go together, and so in history do those of two of the Cambridge spies: Guy Burgess and Donald Maclean.

The two men are forever linked because they defected to the Soviet Union together in 1951 – 'The Missing Diplomats' as Cyril Connolly described them in his book of that name in 1952. And they were Cambridge contemporaries and the two people recruited by Kim Philby for introduction to Arnold Deutsch as NKVD spies back in the 1930s.

Yet, so notoriously debauched and indiscreet was Burgess that, ironically, Maclean spent most of his time as a discreet agent for the USSR as far away from Burgess as possible! One could not really find two more unalike characters. Burgess clearly revelled in his double life, was flamboyant, positively promiscuous, a social butterfly and a regular drinker on an industrial scale of degeneracy.

Maclean, on the other hand, retained much of the puritanism of his Presbyterian ancestry, was fastidious, and only started on a life of drink and sexual adventure when the massive psychological strain of being a traitor began to take its inevitable mental toll. There is, in some ways, something almost honourable in Maclean, a spy out of the profoundest Marxist conviction, while the word 'honour' and Guy Burgess can hardly be contemplated together.

So the two spies who are forever bracketed together were, in reality, very different people, put in the same thought both by their recruitment by Philby and then by their common flight. Burgess and Philby went together, as we saw, much to Philby's disadvantage in 1951. And but for Burgess there might have been no Blunt the spy. But 'Burgess and Maclean'? Only by mistake, as we shall see...

In this chapter I shall consider one of them first, then the other, and end by how they both escaped in 1951, and the very different tales of their subsequent life in the USSR.

Let us first look at Guy Francis de Moncy Burgess, born on 11th April 1911, the son of a naval officer who died when his young son turned thirteen. Burgess was educated at Eton, Britain's most socially privileged school (David Cameron and Prince William being the current best-known alumni) and he then gained a scholarship to Trinity College, providing that august institution with its third spy in a row. Kim Philby once said that Burgess was the best historian he knew and, while one does not naturally associate great learning with Burgess' name, there is little doubting his formidable intellectual abilities, however wasted by drink and partying they soon were – he went from first class honours in part one of the Cambridge History tripos to an aegrotat in his finals, a Latin term for a degree class given to someone who is ill, and in his case surely partly self-inflicted.

But, despite his sad academic record, he managed to get a brief teaching fellowship – he was supposed to do a PhD in history, which was never finished – and above all he became, through Blunt, a member of the Apostles, that self-selecting and rather self-regarding secret coterie that we saw in the Blunt chapter. And here again the fact that many members of that elite were gay is surely irrelevant to treason, and Burgess is once again the exception rather than the rule.

But he was not immune to what another Cambridge contemporary saw as the massive wave of communism sweeping through the university in the early 1930s. While it is difficult to pinpoint his exact conversion to the cause, it is clear that at Cambridge he was one of the many in the emotional tide that persuaded so many young men from privileged backgrounds such as his that they should join the party of the proletariat.

Not that he and others of his kind actually spent much real time with ordinary members of the working class... This was the thing that Robert Cecil, a patriotic Cambridge graduate and long-time colleague of Donald Maclean noticed most about the converts to communism during this period. Beyond joining a march to a nearby town and helping on a strike, not much joint activity took place between the socially elite students and their working class neighbours.

Burgess went from Marxism to treason in May 1934, when he was introduced to 'Otto', alias Arnold Deutsch, and as commentators have rightly pointed out, Deutsch's 'sex-pol' libertarian views on sexual issues, alongside his communist ideologies, would naturally have appealed to a libertine such as Burgess. Being both gay and a spy meant living two clandestine lives at the same time, both being illegal, and this appealed greatly to the histrionic side of Burgess' personality.

Like both Philby and Blunt, Burgess was told by Deutsch to avoid any hint of Marxism or suspicious behaviour that might link him to Communism and thus to his espionage activities on behalf of the USSR. So, as well as giving supposed investment advice to Lady Rothschild (the mother of his good friend Victor) – as if someone from so financially acute family would need his wisdom – he also became secretary to an extremely right-wing Conservative MP, Captain Jack Macnamara. Both Burgess and Macnamara were gay – although it was unlawful, gay men with establishment connections could usually get away with it so long as they did not scare the horses – and, on a visit the two of them made to Nazi Germany with the Anglo-German Fellowship, they spent most of their time finding gay members of the Hitler Youth. One could say that Burgess' attempt to hide his true political colours were if anything going far too far in the opposite direction.

Then, in October 1936, he was able to penetrate the outer edges of the British elite. He was appointed to the BBC Talks Department, then by far one of the most outstanding parts of the media's inner circle. His access to almost anyone would be guaranteed, and being with the BBC gave superb cover. Everyone who was anyone gave BBC talks in those days, and he was able to meet all those who counted in 1930s British society and politics, as well as in the worlds of literature and the arts.

Then, in late 1938, came his entry into the secret world, for which his Soviet controllers had been hoping. He was recruited for what was then called Section D of MI6, renamed in 1940 to the much better-known name of SOE: the Special Operations Executive. Strictly speaking Section D/SOE was *not* about spying, but about destroying as much of the enemy's infrastructure as possible once war began – which it did within ten months of Burgess' recruitment. Indeed, during the Second World War, SOE and MI6 were effectively rivals, MI6 wanting quiet espionage done with no one noticing while SOE was charging around countries such as France blowing up as much as possible and creating deliberate mayhem wherever it went, often at the cost of hideous German reprisals against the local people. But this was in the future – in 1938 Section D was still within MI6, and they had now unwittingly admitted their first Soviet NKVD spy...

Here again, the Nazi-Soviet Pact of August 1939 should have caused Burgess to reconsider his treachery, now that the whole point of being a Soviet spy (the struggle against fascism) was upended by Stalin's *de facto* alliance with Hitler. But, as with the other traitors, this seismic event, communists collaborating with Nazis against the democracies, made no difference, whatever the fictional descriptions of Burgess on television and elsewhere might suggest. He was, like the other Cambridge spies, now a double traitor, a spy for the ally of Britain's enemy Germany.

Burgess was in danger of being called up to fight – as a homosexual he had an excuse not to respond to any summons, the reason for this being that such activity was then illegal. And by now his drinking, always a major problem for him, was getting far worse; an addiction that he was never in the end to solve. By this time, the sheer stress of fourteen-hour days, and (as with his now housemate and fellow spy Anthony Blunt) of living a double life in more than one sense, was taking its toll. In 1940 he totalled a War Office vehicle, while completely drunk in charge, and was immediately sacked.

Now Blunt came to his rescue. He managed to get Burgess into MI5, against the very strong misgivings of John Curry, the head of F Division. And here the conspiracy theorists begin to have a field day. For the person who supported Blunt, and thus overruled Curry in admitting Burgess to MI5, was Guy Liddell, a former officer and now one of the very senior members of the Security Service.

We now know that Liddell was nothing other than a patriotic Englishman. But along with others, such as his equally loyal compatriot and wartime colleague Roger Ellis, he has been accused of being a Soviet spy – if not the Fifth Man, then perhaps the sixth or seventh! For years this devoted MI5 officer was suspected and calumnied, until conclusive proof came from KGB defectors that he was, as he really had been, totally innocent.

Yet he was clearly unwise. People may not make bad decisions out of treachery, but his appointment of Burgess to the inner sanctums of British intelligence was clearly foolish, if only in retrospect. Liddell was unhappily married and soon found himself mixing in the same louche circles as

Blunt and Burgess, becoming part of their social set in their Victor Rothschild-owned apartment in central London. (And as we saw, poor Lord Rothschild was also to be strongly suspected because of these same social links with the two spies.) In 1951, when Burgess and Maclean defected, Liddell had to confess to Curry that the latter had been right after all – that Burgess' appointment was indeed a 'catastrophe'.

Then in 1944 he was admitted to the Foreign Office, where his fellow traitor Donald Maclean was working, but at a much higher level than Burgess, who was placed in the News Department.

This was, however, to be his foot in the door for, in 1946, he gained a much more important and confidential post, that of private secretary to Hector McNeil, the minister of state (and effective political number two to the secretary of state, Ernest Bevin). In this job all kinds of vital policy decisions would cross Burgess' desk, and he would have been able to give vital insights into the thinking of the British government (and after its formation in 1949, that of NATO as well) to his Soviet controllers.

Worse still, he was made head of a brand new Information Research Department. Like many such organisations, this was not as it appeared – it was, in effect, to discover what Soviet propaganda was trying to do in the new Cold War battle of ideas, and combat it as rigorously as possible.

The irony of a Soviet spy being in charge of such a department is of course obvious! This was the same as Philby being in charge of counter-intelligence against the NKVD while at MI6, and thus equally damaging to British interests, as all that the United Kingdom (and after 1949 its NATO allies) were trying to do to counter the very powerful Soviet propaganda machine was being guided by one of their own agents!

Thankfully his continued outrageous personal behaviour, on foreign trips in line with his duties, soon meant that he had to be transferred. Drunkenness (and overt and indiscreet homosexual activity) however was seen to be the problem, rather than any kind of treachery – indeed it was almost a shield against his being exposed as a traitor, since who would possibly want to recruit someone as utterly wild as him?

But his transfer could not have come at a better time for his Soviet controllers. For he was now placed in the Far Eastern Department of the Foreign Office – just in the build-up and early days of the Korean War! The American commander General MacArthur always felt that there was someone malign in supposed allied countries, leaking material to the USSR and, as we now know, he was entirely right: Guy Burgess was keeping the KGB fully informed of western thinking at the most crucial stages of the Korean conflict.

(Indeed this is my one journalistic coup! I found some key documents in Foreign Office archives back in the 1980s, under the 30-Year Rule, that showed quite how much high-grade material Burgess was leaking to the Soviets. The scoop was subsequently published in an article by historian Peter Hennessy in The Times and as a footnote in one of his academic books, for those who wish to look further.)

Then came a fatal move that was, unknown to the Cambridge spies, soon to unmask two of them and make the others effectively redundant.

In August 1950 he was appointed as Second Secretary at the British Embassy in Washington – something that, he admitted to his fellow spy Kim Philby, would be something of 'a shock'.

Indeed it was. In 1949 Burgess had been on a particularly wild and debauched official trip to Gibraltar and Tangiers, where his drunken and indiscreet behaviour had been unusually notorious, even for him. How it could be that, even after that, he was given a sensitive post in Washington DC beggars the imagination – and one of the reasons why Guy Liddell subsequently got into such trouble was that he wrote that while Burgess was wont to be drunk and unwise, he was not the kind of person to give away any secrets while intoxicated!

Whether the inebriated behaviour was a sign of the stress of his two double lives – Soviet spy/Foreign Office official and gay man in a legally straight world – is difficult to know, though the issue has been much speculated. As his massive drinking continued in the USSR after 1951 until his death in 1963, it is possible that he was simply someone with a major drink dependency problem in and of itself, even if he had never been a traitor or if homosexuality had been legalised in Britain, which it was four years after his death. But at this distance it is probably difficult to pronounce conclusively. Whatever the reason, it put him in a dangerous position and, as would now prove to be the case, his friends as well.

Kim Philby always said later that the reason why he asked Burgess to live at his house in DC – to the horror of Philby's politer friends – was to be able to keep an eye on him. Just because Philby was a notorious liar does not make this rationale untrue – but we can say in retrospect that it was only a partial reason now that the details of Philby's treachery are known.

For, as we will see when we look at Maclean, one of the USSR's major problems is that their main NKVD (and soon to be called KGB) agent handler was in New York and not in DC, where surveillance would in any case have been much tighter. It was hard for Maclean and then Philby to have excuses to get down to New York, but this was, it seems, less the case with Burgess, whose official post at the embassy was less important than those held by the other two.

Consequently Burgess was able to act as Philby's go-between with Valeri Makayev, the KGB 'illegal' codenamed HARRY, but who was based in New York. Given the vital importance of the material Philby was giving them – which we saw in another chapter – this conduit was absolutely vital, and Burgess' residence at the Philby family home was ideal cover.

But for all the remaining spies, it was also a disaster.

By now it was known that Donald Maclean was HOMER, the Soviet spy unearthed in the VENONA decrypts. As we saw in the Philby chapter, it was Kim Philby who tipped off his friends in Britain that Maclean was blown. And so now it is time to look at Maclean's story, before concluding with the story that forever linked Burgess and Maclean together in the minds of history.

Donald Maclean was born in London on 25th May 1913. He was a younger son of one of the most eminent liberal politicians of the day, Donald (later on the Rt Hon Sir Donald) Maclean, a lawyer, politician and, at the time of his death in 1932, a member of the national government that ruled the United Kingdom.

Maclean was of strict, rather dour, Presbyterian Scottish ancestry, something with which the psychologists have had a field day, since many of Maclean's hang-ups are attributed to this stern, inflexible and serious upbringing. But, while this is possible, young Donald was actually raised in England, and his father himself was raised, not in Scotland, but in Wales.

By Donald's birth in 1913 his father was Deputy Chairman of Ways and Means in the House of Commons which is, in effect, deputy to the deputy to the actual Speaker of the House of Commons (in Britain, unlike in the USA, a very strictly non-partisan post). Maclean's background was thus one of privilege and material plenty, but because of the severity of it – his family was teetotal for example as well – not at all similar to the more sybaritic childhood at Eton of Guy Burgess and those of aristocratic ancestry.

Similarly, while he went to private school, it was to Gresham's school in Holt, not to Eton or Westminster or Harrow, or a similar school of ancient foundation and parental wealth. Gresham's had a code of honesty, based upon draconian moral precepts that all the boys were expected to follow.

And here, perhaps, some psychological speculation is warranted, including that by Lord Annan, the former

Provost of King's College, Cambridge, who was very much part of the progressive milieu at Cambridge, of Bloomsbury and of *bien pensant* attitudes; yet, as he pointed out in his introduction to Robert Cecil's definitive book on Donald Maclean, *A Divided Life*, very much not a traitor or an apologist for the USSR.

For, as he says, many an atheistic humanist is the son or grandson of Victorian evangelical Christians. It is not so much that they reject an austere lifestyle or set of firm doctrinaire beliefs, but rather that they substitute a new set of their own for those of their parents that they have rejected for themselves.

In terms of Maclean this fascinating insight makes huge sense. Marxism, especially in its Soviet form, was a very strict sect, one demanding absolute obedience to what its protagonists believed totally was unquestionable truth. And in that, as historians throughout the twentieth century have often argued, is really a modern/atheist form of equally dogmatic versions of Christianity which, if one looks at the Jesuits and similar groups in church history, are remarkably similar to the adherents of Marxist-Leninism in our own era.

So, in rejecting the stern presbyterianism of his ancestry, and in rebelling against it and them, Maclean was not casting aside belief in an absolute with unquestioning loyalty, but in effect substituting one overarching and demanding system for another. *What* he believed was completely different from his family, but the *mindset* would seem, I think one can argue, exactly the same.

Thus when he went to Cambridge in the 1930s in the same turbulent political and social/economic upheaval times as his Marxist contemporaries, the attraction to him of the USSR, of Marxism over fascism, of Stalin over Hitler, was one that we have seen before, with Philby, Blunt and Burgess.

And as with them, his allegiance was always more theoretical than practical, writing articles, attending meetings of the Cambridge University Socialist Society, rather than one of actual direct engagement with real-life members of the underprivileged working class.

One small point – he was, like the atomic bomb spy, at Trinity Hall, not Trinity College which is the much bigger and far richer college nearby. Trinity Hall was much older, but also far smaller, less self-aware, nowhere near as wealthy, and with a sense of collegiate intimacy that larger institutions such as Trinity College often lack. It might be easier to conflate the colleges – as they have been by some portraits of the Cambridge spies – but the two colleges in honour of the Holy Trinity are in fact quite separate, something of which all their students would have been aware then as they are now.

Having been recommended by Philby, Maclean (who gained a first class degree in Modern Languages from Cambridge) entered the Diplomatic Service in 1935, the first of the Cambridge spies actually to penetrate the establishment. And it is important to remember that he was only ever an actual spy for the USSR: his job in the Foreign Office was that of a straight diplomat, albeit one on the fast track, with great success expected of him.

And here he had the classic dilemma of a traitor: he had to do well enough at his official job to get promoted and to be someone of consequence whose voice was heard, yet, at the same time, serving the interests of another country and in a way that did not draw suspicion to him. He was to find this increasingly difficult, and his drinking problem, which grew steadily worse while he was living his double existence, can be strongly attributed to the hard time he had – unlike Philby, but more like Blunt, he was not someone to whom duplicity came easily.

Much has been made of the fact that Maclean was bisexual, this being another source of his supposed inner angst. But, in 1940, he met an American student in Paris – he had been posted there to the British Embassy in 1938 as a Third Secretary – called Melinda Marling, the daughter of well-off, divorced American parents. This was by all accounts a very happy marriage, and one of the things that we now know for certain is that he took the astonishing step of informing her about his double life, working for the British but actually also for Moscow, when he married her. (Whether this made her a communist as well is not known, but she certainly never betrayed him to the authorities.) They married just as the Germans were coming – the fact that Melinda was pregnant (with a child who sadly did not survive birth later in the year) may well have been a contributing factor, as well as the imminent arrival of the Wehrmacht in Paris.

It is true that at that time many gay people married because that is what was expected of them, when their inner leanings were still illegal. But by all accounts theirs was a genuine marriage and happy for much of the time, until Melinda finally betrayed him, not to the British or Americans, but in Moscow and to Kim Philby, after 1963 and after twenty years of marriage.

It is also said that he suppressed his homosexuality, or his inclinations in that direction. Again it is hard to know, and one wonders whether, with Maclean, as opposed to Burgess and Blunt, it really was a factor at all in his loyalty to the USSR and to the communist cause. It could well be that with him sexual issues were separate from ideological, and so to emphasise his bisexuality in relation to his treachery is a canard.

During the 1939 to 1941 period he, like the other Cambridge spies, was a double traitor, since this was, as we saw, the period of the Nazi-Soviet Pact: he was giving information in 1940 to the USSR's *de facto* ally Germany, as the Wehrmacht was invading France. Since, in 1940, Britain and France contemplated going to war with the USSR to defend Finland against Soviet aggression, Stalin would have been even more paranoid about the western allies, and he would have known all about such plans from Maclean. Even a lowly Third Secretary was capable of great damage to his homeland.

In 1940 he was back in the Foreign Office, during the worst of the blitz, which caused endless suffering to the young Macleans as well as to millions of others in London. Melinda went home to have the baby, but when it died she would come home and rejoin Donald, still in London.

He was very careful to stay away from his louche Cambridge friends – contrary to legend and myth he kept as far away from Burgess and Blunt as possible, though he did meet up with Philby, now with SOE, in 1940, to re-establish links with their mutual controller in the Soviet Embassy. And it should be said that the fact that Burgess and Blunt lived in the same house and socialised in identical circles was a breach of all NKVD rules, as were Philby's links to them. Maclean, in keeping a far distance, was obeying Moscow rules on how agents in the field should behave.

Maclean was in the General Department, a catch-all kind of place in the Foreign Office, much of it to do with what was then called 'economic warfare' (which had its own ministry and which, politically, controlled SOE – to the annoyance of those in MI6). Another subject was shipping, none of these being issues about which Maclean knew much – the cult of the gentleman amateur still reigned in the Foreign Office.

He was very lucky to be in any kind of post at all. A defector just before the war broke out, Walter Krivitsky, had fled the USSR and had first gone to the Canadians. Krivitsky was to be murdered in mysterious circumstances in the USA in 1941 and, while it has never been proved, it is more than likely that someone in Britain or the USA betrayed him. (We should not forget that there were Soviet spies in the United States as well, including Treasury official Henry Dexter White and leading diplomat Alger Hiss.)

Krivitsky had mentioned an aristocratic Scot, educated at Eton and Oxford, and with bohemian tastes. This was clearly *not* Donald Maclean, whose ancestry was Scottish but who was raised in England and at Gresham's school and Cambridge. But, in retrospect, it is possible to see that there was a misunderstanding about Maclean's background, and that the person whom Krivitsky had named on his trip to Britain in 1940 was indeed Maclean himself.

Then, in 1944, his career took a massive upward turn – he was named as an official at the British Embassy in Washington DC. During the four years in which he was to be there he was to inflict incalculable damage on the west, and perhaps more than any of the other Cambridge spies, as what he was able to accomplish for his Soviet controllers arguably made a major difference to the course of the early Cold War.

Contrary to what was previously believed, Maclean, who soon got promoted to First Secretary at the embassy, was involved very early on in the British-American talks on atomic weapons, certainly as early as 1945, and in time for Stalin to know all about it *before* the Americans told the Soviet leader of the bomb's existence at the Yalta conference at the beginning of that year.

Since Melinda Maclean was mainly in New York with her family – the children were growing in number all the time – Maclean had the perfect opportunity to see his Soviet controller without the beady eyes of security in Washington DC upon him, though it is thought that, in the capital, he used dead letter drops, and in one case had a meeting with Alger Hiss, who was very early on exposed as a Soviet spy. (Hiss denied it at the time, but the VENONA decrypts that exposed Maclean as early as 1951 later made it certain beyond doubt that Hiss, then a leading diplomat, was an NKVD agent as well.)

As Maclean's then contemporary in Washington (and subsequent biographer) Robert Cecil has written, Maclean was seen in DC as the coming man. (Cecil was, for a while, the Foreign Office designated assistant to 'C', the Head of MI6, and was now in the embassy with Maclean.) And what Cecil says is significant, since to me it suggests that Maclean was a far more important spy than myth would have it, giving that eminence to Philby instead.

While it is true that Philby could have become Head of MI6, it is equally the case that Maclean could have become Head of the Diplomatic Service. For, when the VENONA decrypts first suggested that there was a Soviet mole in the British Embassy, the other possible suspect short-listed was someone called Paul Gore-Booth. As we now know, Gore-Booth was a total patriot and entirely innocent. But what is interesting is that he, a contemporary of Maclean in DC, did end up as Lord Gore-Booth, and as Head of the Diplomatic Service. But for VENONA that person could have been Maclean...

For, as Cecil points out, when Maclean was still in Washington the idea that he was a permanently drunken, promiscuous homosexual is total rubbish – that might have been entirely true of Burgess, but certainly not of Maclean. Whenever extra work needed doing, Maclean was always the one chosen, because of his intelligence and competence (and his tennis playing skills did not go amiss...). If he had been then as he was to become in Cairo and in later portrayals of him, none of this would have been even thinkable. One does not give atomic secrets to drunken sots.

And, ironically, *so* secret were the atomic discussions that, not merely were most of the British Embassy staff unaware of them, but so too, at Prime Minister Attlee's insistence, were most of the British Cabinet! But, thanks to Maclean, Stalin knew all the secrets, which many senior British diplomats and politicians did not!

In 1947 Maclean was able to enter the inner sanctum itself, as Joint Secretary to the Anglo-American-Canadian Combined Policy Committee on the atomic bomb and uranium supplies.

Furthermore, Stalin knew one major secret that we now know made a huge difference to how the Soviet Union behaved during the early years of the Cold War – and again all thanks to Maclean.

While the USA and Britain got atomic bombs first, they had precious little uranium. Consequently it has now emerged that in the first period of the Cold War they had not nearly as many atomic weapons as they would have liked, and certainly far fewer than they would have preferred the Soviets to think that they had. Not only that but Maclean, in one of his duties, had to find out how many western forces there were aligned against a possible Russian invasion force. Thus Stalin, in formulating Soviet policy towards the USA (before the creation of NATO in 1949) knew (a) exactly how many atomic bombs the USA *really* possessed and (b) where and how many the US forces were to defend the west against a Soviet-bloc invasion.

It could not have been better if he had tried, and, in addition, Beria, the head of the NKVD, was also the person in charge of the Soviet atomic weapons research organisation, so what Maclean was passing on was doubly helpful.

And, finally, Maclean was one of the very few people – American let alone British like him – allowed with unrestricted access to the brand new American Atomic Energy Commission, a privilege that he apparently used on many occasions.

But all good things come to an end, and in 1948 Maclean was posted to Cairo, as the Counsellor in the British Embassy to Egypt.

Then, since Britain effectively controlled that country until the overthrow of the corrupt monarchy in 1952, that posting was far more important than it is now, with the Suez Canal still in Anglo-French hands and much of the Middle East in the British zone of influence, and the brand new state of Israel not nearly as powerful as it is now. And, interestingly, back in 1948 the USA was nowhere near as Zionist as it has since become. Israel had a strong left-wing tradition among its founders, and so the Soviet Union rather than the USA was, in those very early days, the country to whom Israel would have looked for support. As for the Foreign Office, both it and the Foreign Secretary, Ernest Bevin, were strongly pro-Arab.

Therefore the move to Cairo was certainly not a demotion but another part in Maclean's upward rise and he was the youngest person of his rank in the Foreign Office.

But it is clearly here that his double life began to unravel, and to do so spectacularly.

On one occasion he and his old friend Philip Toynbee completely smashed up the private apartment of some American diplomats and, on another, he injured a fellow British diplomat on a cruise down the Nile. His alcohol levels now really were rising, and it is from his drunken and wild behaviour in Cairo that the legend about him derives its origins.

Several things were, of course, wrong; his double life surely the chief cause of his decline. He once told a friend that being a spy was like cleaning a lavatory: a nasty job but someone had to do it. People who knew him well have written that, unlike Burgess and especially unlike Philby, Maclean never really enjoyed being a secret agent – he did it not for the fun of being a spy but because of his absolute beliefs in the rightness of the communist cause.

And now Melinda was emerging from her cocoon, becoming not a wallflower but an active hostess, with the Maclean household filled with parties and visitors, especially those from the Egyptian elite, including not a few men who rather admired Melinda. None of this was pleasant for Maclean and, as someone with a secret life to hide, he must have felt rather claustrophobic as time progressed.

The smashing up of the room in 1950 was too much even for the Foreign Office, which was, as many historians and commentators have since agreed, rather too lenient to bad behaviour in its own ranks (how otherwise could someone as outrageous as Burgess ever have survived a single day in many other institutions?) Maclean was sent back for therapy in England and Melinda and the children spent some time abroad on holiday.

Maclean was careful not to have the official Foreign Office psychologist on his case since, of course, the main reason for his bizarre behaviour and depression was his treachery – although the change in marital dynamics was an influence and one to which he could have admitted to colleagues and superiors.

Instead he chose a rather outlandish Jungian psychiatrist, a Dr Rose, otherwise properly called Dr Erna Rosenbaum. Today this would create suspicion, since her links and background could well have been suspect. But, in that more innocent age, she was acceptable and soon Maclean was able to unburden all his admissible foibles: his closet homosexuality (or perhaps bisexuality might be more appropriate in his case), his marriage and other pressures. Whether or not he admitted his deepest issue – his treachery – is not known. Certainly he unleashed on those who truly knew his secret, attacking, for example, Goronwy Rees, who had been a Marxist back in the 1930s but had long since thought better of betraying his country.

But we do know the extraordinary reaction of the Foreign Office who, in the autumn of 1950 actually promoted Maclean to the highly influential and confidential post of Head of the American Department! He was already under suspicion as being HOMER, the spy named in the VENONA decrypts, and he was well aware that somebody was now tailing him.

Eventually he ceased to be given truly top-secret documents, which was another indication to him that he was under suspicion. How much damage he was able to do here at his last post is hard to assess, since much of the most-secret part of the Anglo-US relationship was now dealt with by other Foreign Office departments (such as NATO), but even so he would still have been in a position to pass on all sorts of very secret documents to his NKVD controllers, especially since this was also the time of the beginning of the Korean War.

But as his fellow diplomat Robert Cecil has written, perhaps the worst legacy he left was the grave damage to US-UK relations when the Americans found out that he and Burgess were really NKVD agents, and had been for a long time. So horrified was the US establishment at what they regarded as outrageous laxity in security by the Foreign Office and intelligence services that trust between the USA and UK took a long time to re-establish – and as we saw in the chapter on Philby, the overreaction of James Jesus Angleton was to wreak vast damage within the CIA as well, and for decades to come.

We will look at Maclean's flight with Burgess to Moscow in 1951 in the next part of this chapter. What is interesting is how he behaved when he got to Moscow. Burgess drank himself to death and, as for Philby, once he sobered up and found sympathetic members of the KGB with whom to relate such as Yuri Modin, he soon got back into intelligence work, but this time working overtly for his Soviet spymasters.

Not so Maclean who, once he was able to come in from hiding and live publicly in Moscow, resumed life as a family man and became, in effect, an academic, working especially closely with the Institute of World Economics and International Relations, right up until his death in 1983. His private life was tragic, since Melinda soon deserted him for Philby, and his children decided that they wanted to go and live back in the west, for which choice one cannot blame them.

Rather than write self-promoting memoirs, as Philby did, Maclean instead wrote an academic textbook, *British Foreign Policy Since Suez*, published in Britain in 1970 and which experts regard as being genuinely written by Maclean himself. Friends say that he was most unhappy about the abuse of psychiatric prisons to control dissidents and, while he was loyal unto the end to the communist cause, the idea of a former spy and traitor being sympathetic to Soviet dissidents is certainly an interesting one. Similarly it seems that he was horrified at the latent anti-Semitism of the USSR in this period, again a form of dissent that distinguished him strongly from Philby, whose sycophancy to the KGB stands in very vivid contrast.

He died on the 6th March 1983. But his ashes are in the family graveyard in Buckinghamshire, alongside his parents, the very bourgeois people against whom he rebelled yet with whom he now lies in death. If any of the Cambridge spies could be said to be honourable – and it is hard to know if one can ever use such a term for someone who betrayed his country – it is surely Donald Maclean.

Much nonsense has been written about how he and Burgess slipped out of Britain and successfully to Moscow in 1951. Some of it has been speculation, and some, without doubt, KGB misinformation, especially Philby's rather mendacious memoirs. But a main reason is that, until the archives were examined by historians after 2002, we simply have not known what actually happened. We can now find out what both the Soviet and British secret archives reveal, and a far better understanding of the real events is now possible – in so much as a limited glimpse into intelligence material can never tell us the whole truth, since surely there is much that remains concealed even more than six decades after the events at which we now look.

So what follows is inevitably partial, but I think, as near as we will ever get, and I think that what we shall now investigate might actually be the genuine article! At least we can hope so.

The old version was that, once Philby realised that the Americans had correctly named HOMER as Maclean, it was vital to get Maclean out of Britain as fast as possible, lest he blab and reveal the full nature of the Cambridge spy ring. So he told Burgess, who was with him in Washington DC, to get so outrageously drunk and abusive, and so physically destructive with a car, that he had to be sent home to rescue Maclean and abscond with the latter to the USSR.

(Another, hitherto plausible version, by people who knew the Cambridge ring, is that, so embarrassing a liability had Burgess become, that Philby was desperate to get his leaky and debauched colleague back to London and out of DC as soon as possible. But this is now unlikely, as we shall discover.)

In fact we now know that the Philby version, while having an element of truth in it, is in reality not the entire story. Furthermore the declassification of CIA and MI5, as well as Russian KGB archives is only one way of knowing. For we have several other, non-official corroborative sources...

First there were the interviews given by Kim Philby to the top investigative journalist Phillip Knightley, but several years after Philby's own rather mendacious memoirs. Then there was the interview done by a Russian journalist a while afterwards, Genrikh Borovik, who was later on able to compare and contrast what Philby told him with what was actually in Philby's own KGB file, which, amazingly, Borovik was able to consult. The former senior KGB officer Yuri Modin has spilled some beans in his own autobiography. And Christopher Andrew has now told us what MI5 knew at the time and what he has discovered since from defectors such as Oleg Gordievsky.

But what of these is the truth? As both Knightley and Borovik remind us, there is much we will never know, since it is unlikely that the KGB will ever *fully* spill its inner secrets. Especially since the defection of Burgess and

Maclean, while looking, at that time in 1951, like a major success for the Soviets, was, in the long term, a total disaster; a short-term gain for an ultimate major loss.

So let us try to reconstruct things as an amalgam of these sources suggests might well have been the case – and which certainly makes much sense in retrospect, over sixty years later, with the Cold War over and the Soviet Union no longer in existence.

Maclean had been blown, as we shall see. But how about his fellow traitor, Guy Burgess – surely there is a good case for saying that he was equally burned out as well, and was thus, from the Soviet point of view, an equal liability?

There are those who argue that Maclean could possibly have brazened it out, rather as Philby was able to do until 1963, and as Blunt succeeded in doing for even longer. But, given his delicate temperament, this is rather unlikely. There is an excellent argument for saying that Burgess' condition was equally shaky, as his drink dependency was worsening.

And here we need to get rid of the first myth: that Burgess deliberately got himself expelled from Washington DC in order to go back and warn Maclean that the VENONA decrypts had revealed all. The new thinking – and it is surely correct – is that Burgess' exploits were a Foreign Office excuse to send him home, rather than a manufactured opportunity to get back to Britain without raising suspicion. Certainly, when Philby saw that Maclean was exposed as HOMER, he and Burgess got together to plot what next to do – but it was taking advantage of Burgess already being sent home in disgrace, rather than the foreordained plot that Philby wanted it to be seen as when he wrote his memoirs.

For, as Philby knew, if Burgess was exposed as a Soviet agent, then he, Philby, as his landlord in DC and Cambridge contemporary would be immediately under suspicion. The importance of this cannot be exaggerated. If Burgess and Maclean – his Cambridge cohorts – were *both* spies for Moscow, then Philby's own position would be highly exposed. Since Philby thought of himself as a future Director of MI6 – and plenty of other unsuspecting fellow members of the British establishment also saw him in that favourable light – then anything that might blow his chances of the ultimate prize would be truly catastrophic. Imagine it – the Head of MI6 a KGB spy! Nothing could possibly come in the way of something as extraordinary as that.

So we come on now to the next new hypothesis: Philby wanted Burgess only to warn Maclean, not go to Moscow with him. For as Miranda Carter, Blunt's biographer, and others suggest, even if Burgess only went as far as, say, Paris, with Maclean, it would be very difficult to explain even that to the British authorities if Maclean, as planned, ended up in Moscow.

Burgess, as we have just seen, was often the messenger for Philby to the KGB. I think that it is likely that Philby only saw him now in the same respect, as a mere messenger, but certainly not as a defector to the USSR with Maclean. For, contrary to how the Cambridge spies are often portrayed in the media, Burgess and Maclean had, in 1951, not seen each other for years. And Maclean was at Trinity Hall not at Trinity College, and if only Maclean vanished, then Philby would not be under suspicion. But in 1951 Burgess and Philby, who had been in the same college at Cambridge, had clearly known each other for years, and shared a house in Washington DC, evidently had the very closest of ties. The defection of *Burgess* to the USSR would spell disaster, as Philby surely knew.

I think therefore that *Plan A was for Burgess to tell Maclean to defect but stay himself in Britain*, maybe with a new job, perhaps one outside the secret world but perhaps in something that would still give him access to decent secrets, such as being a journalist. (We know he contacted the Berry family, then owners of *The Daily Telegraph*, for possible work.)

However the Soviets knew something that Philby probably knew inside but might not have wanted to admit: that Burgess was as washed up and burned out as Maclean. His days as a spy of any real use were over.

Somewhere therefore – perhaps in Moscow or maybe in the KGB residency in London – the plan changed. Burgess was not just to warn Maclean but to escort him to Moscow.

Yuri Modin has admitted that, in retrospect, this was a monumental mistake of prime order. It would have been, he concedes decades later and with hindsight, much better to let Maclean go on his own and tail him to ensure that he got to Moscow safely. This way Burgess would never have been suspected and, with Burgess in the clear, Philby would have been as well. For remember, contrary to legend, Burgess and Maclean, the two spies always linked together, had not in reality been in touch for years.

Thus in the end, the disastrous decision was made: Burgess would not merely warn Maclean but would take him all the way to Moscow, which is what we now know is exactly what happened.

But there is a further twist for it now seems that Burgess was not expecting to stay in Moscow but actually to come home! Looking back now over sixty years later this seems utterly incredible, but there is good evidence to suggest that this was precisely the case. And since Blunt resolutely refused to go when asked, one can see that Burgess only went because he thought he was coming back, however ludicrously unlikely this would now seem in practice.

And as Philby foresaw, Burgess' defection immediately shone the light on him, effectively ending Philby's career in MI6, and most assuredly destroying forever his chances of becoming Head of MI6 and the most important Soviet agent in history. With Burgess gone as well as Maclean, those who had long suspected Philby began to have the ammunition they needed and, while it took until 1963 to finally prove Philby's guilt, his meteoric rise was now over.

Burgess never really adapted to life in the USSR. His drinking problems persisted right until the end, in 1963, and were almost certainly a major contributory factor to his death. There was a brief canard he was able to trail, letting the authorities in Britain think for a short while that he wanted to come home but, in truth, however homesick he may have been, he knew full well that only prison could await him if he really had returned, to inevitable arrest, prosecution and sentence.

His friend, the maverick (and also gay) Labour MP Tom Driberg wrote a brief life on him, rather ludicrously trying to deny Burgess' years of espionage (as if there had been another reason to go to Moscow). Once the MI5 secret archives were unlocked, it emerged that Driberg, while not a direct spy in the way Burgess and others had been, nonetheless was what the KGB would call 'an agent of influence' – someone painting a rosy picture of the USSR, or what Lenin, perhaps more accurately, referred to as a 'useful idiot'.

Burgess died unreconciled with Philby, who blamed Burgess for his eventual exposure. But I rather agree with those who say that Burgess was a substitute for Philby's rage against those who had *really* betrayed him – their mutual KGB bosses, who compelled Burgess to stay in 1951. Borovik is right: Philby was essentially blown by his own masters once Burgess was uncovered as well as Maclean.

Burgess and Maclean were two very different kinds of spy. Both did huge damage to Britain. But perhaps in fleeing in 1951, thereby unmasking Philby, they actually did their country a favour, as Philby's meteoric rise in MI6 was over, even if he was not finally unmasked in a provable way until his own flight to Moscow in 1963. From such a fate – a KGB agent as Head of MI6 – Burgess and Maclean spared us.

THE SECRETS OF THE ATOM

John Cairncross and Alan Nunn May

Who or what killed Princess Diana? Was it the fact that she was not wearing a seat belt or was it a plot by dark forces to remove her from the scene?

This might seem an unlikely link to the two spies in this chapter but, in fact, there is one – it is conspiracy theory. Do secret agencies like MI5 tell the truth or are they always liars? Was it al-Qaida who destroyed the Twin Towers in 2001 or was it a plot by Mossad and the CIA?

Obviously intelligence services need to keep secrets – otherwise they could not operate properly. But are they *never* honest? Churchill famously said that truth was so important that it had to be surrounded by a 'bodyguard of lies' and much of the derring-do and deception planning in the Second World War did exactly that, with, what we now know, to be enormously beneficial effect on D-day, when the Germans fully expected the invasion to come at Calais, not in Normandy, because of an immensely successful disinformation campaign organised to deceive them by British intelligence.

But does this automatically make MI5 and its historians into liars?

I rather think not and, in the case of the first of our spies, we also have evidence from the former Soviet Union that backs up the MI5 version of history, and with no benefit to the USSR. For, in John Cairncross, we have an odd example: a spy who, unlike his Trinity contemporary Kim Philby, deliberately underplayed his importance as a spy, in what MI5 historian Christopher Andrew has surely rightly called his mendacious memoirs, *The Enigma Spy*. In that book Cairncross does the opposite of Philby: instead of grossly exaggerating his role as a spy, he dismisses himself as someone of little importance, and whose only contribution to espionage was actually a good one, sending our Soviet ally information from Enigma in 1943 that helped the Red Army beat the Germans at Kursk, the biggest tank battle in history.

But how much of the John Cairncross version is true? I think that there is far too much myth, and indeed more so than even the MI5 official history is able to expose, since much about him is exaggerated and, as Christopher Andrew proved, along with former KGB officer Yuri Modin, actually untrue.

There are two legends – one, that he was, in effect, a socially awkward working-class oik; the second, that he never really betrayed his country as all he was doing was helping Britain's ally, the USSR.

We shall see later on why the second scenario is false.

With the first, this is certainly what was implied about him. Another Trinity man, Sir Jock Colville, of impeccable aristocratic lineage and later a secretary first to Winston Churchill during the war and afterwards, and in between to Queen Elizabeth II when heiress to the throne, once said of Cairncross, when interrogated by MI5, that he 'was very brilliant but very boring'. Sir Stuart Hampshire, later a senior Oxford academic (and at one time himself thought to be a traitor but later proved to be innocent) was even more damning:

'He was an absurd and rather untidy scholar, bright and academic. He was socially from the lower rather than the higher, very talkative, sort of chaotic.'

This is, of course, pure snobbery. Cairncross was born in Scotland on 25th July 1913. His father was an ironmonger, his mother a schoolteacher. But it was hardly a rough-hewn background. Most accounts of him omit his brother, and this is interesting. Sir Alec Cairncross, born two years earlier in 1911 went, like his brother John, to Glasgow University. But then Alec went to Cambridge, where he would have overlapped with his brother – there were *two* Cairncrosses at Cambridge at this time, not just one – and gained the second-ever PhD in economics, and was part of the John Maynard Keynes circle (and of other economists such as James Meade). After a distinguished wartime career he was a professor at the University of Glasgow (of which he was very proudly Chancellor from 1972 to 1976) and then went back to work for the government. In 1964, the year in which his brother John confessed to being a spy for the NKVD, Alec was made Head of the Government Economic

Service, retiring in 1969 with a knighthood and with the mastership of a college at Oxford, where he died in 1998.

His daughter (and thus John's niece), Frances, is also distinguished in her own right, having been a very successful journalist for *The Guardian* and then *The Economist*. She is one of the first women to be head of a formerly all-male college at Oxford: she is Rector of Exeter College, a post formerly held by Lord Trend after his retirement as Secretary to the Cabinet (and known in intelligence circles as the man who investigated whether or not Sir Roger Hollis of MI5 was a Soviet agent).

So, despite Sir Stuart Hampshire's condescension, it is possible that John Cairncross was a rather awkward and maybe even socially inept person, but then so too can be individuals of all kinds of social backgrounds, from the aristocratic to the economically deprived. Alec Cairncross had no problems with fitting in, both at Cambridge as a Glaswegian, and as a state-educated Scot in wartime, and later peacetime, Whitehall. Any problems that John Cairncross had can thus be attributed to him purely personally rather than the snobbish disdain that Colville and Hampshire echoed towards him. But it could be, as has been suggested, that John Cairncross, unlike his brother, had a huge chip on his shoulder, in which case he would have perceived insults where none existed. Perhaps this was the case. For Burgess'/Blunt's working-class lover Jack Hewit, who shared a "lower" social background with Cairncross, apparently found him truly "dull". So it is possible then, that the *perception* of dislike could have been a triggering factor in Cairncross' dislike of the privileged classes, and part of his eventual rationale for treachery.

Clever Cairncross most certainly was, though.

After gaining a degree, like his brother, from the University of Glasgow, he went on to study in Paris at the Sorbonne, which was still directly connected to the famous French university founded in the middle ages (and broken up in 1970). From there he gained the prestigious Bell Exhibition to Trinity College, Cambridge, where he managed to gain his degree in two years instead of the normal three.

It was at Cambridge that he met Anthony Blunt, by this time a fellow of Trinity, and it is here that the controversy about Cairncross' life begins.

In his memoirs, *The Enigma Spy*, he professes strong dislike of Blunt and all of that particular social set with whom, aesthetically and in terms of sexual preference, he would have nothing in common. (But remember, Kim Philby was straight, and at the heart of the conspiracy.) He had occasional supervisions in French from Blunt, whose expertise on linguistics he disdained.

However, the fact that Jack Hewit knew him well enough to find him boring – and this would have been well after Cambridge – shows that Cairncross must have known the Blunt–Burgess ménage during the war. And as we have seen, it was Maclean who was careful to keep his distance, so as to avoid suspicion.

Cairncross confesses to have been actively communist at Cambridge and to have been part of the circle of the overtly communist Cambridge intellectual, James Klugmann.

Klugmann is interesting, since he was never reticent about being an open communist and was able, despite this, to work for SOE during the Second World War. He was among those, including the decidedly non-communist Conservative MP, Sir Fitzroy Maclean (no relative of Donald), to argue for supporting Tito's communist partisans to back against the Germans in Yugoslavia rather than the Royalist Cetniks. For the Ultra decrypts revealed that the latter were doing nothing like as much to combat the axis forces as the partisans. (And it was Churchill who took that controversial decision, for short-term British reasons, knowing Tito's Communist sympathies full well.)

Was Klugmann an actual spy though? No one seems to think so, and it is possible that he was someone who was passionately communist without actually betraying his country – he would only deal with Soviet agents through the official apparatus of the Communist Party of Great Britain rather than directly as a secret agent for the NKVD. This may be splitting hairs but he may be an interesting example of someone who could espouse Marxism but not the Soviet Union as a state to be supported against his own country.

This is all relevant to how, exactly, Cairncross was recruited, and to the myths that he tried to create about himself.

His own version is that he was recruited as a spy in a kind of trap, with a reluctant Klugmann doing the introductions in a park in London (the same place where Philby was recruited) to 'Otto', who we now know from Philby's story was Arnold Deutsch, an NKVD 'illegal'.

However, although Cairncross and Klugmann knew each other, this account has now been shown to be total fiction – and from the investigation of Soviet sources as well as British secret archives. Cairncross was recommended to the NKVD – to 'Otto'/Arnold Deutsch – by Blunt himself, and was recruited, not on a park bench but in Cambridge, on a visit there by Guy Burgess, whom Cairncross later admitted to knowing and liking, even though, of course, what could be said about Blunt could equally be said about Burgess, whose social background was, if anything, even more privileged than Blunt's.

So already the myths are becoming seen for what they are.

And, swiftly, Cairncross proved himself to be an ideal agent in the right place and at the right time. Indeed his Soviet controllers, who would not have shared the social snobberies of a Colville or a Hampshire, thought very highly indeed of him – one later very senior KGB officer stating that he was as good as Philby, their star recruit.

For, in 1936, his sheer brain power paid dividends – he came top of all the entrants not just for the Foreign Office but also for the Home Civil Service (in those days separate entities). This was a remarkable achievement by any account.

In some ways it was odd that he chose the Foreign Office – unless it was that his Soviet controllers, not knowing the minutiae of the British class system, felt that was where he should go. His social awkwardness made him stand out strongly in the smooth and silky atmosphere there and both Donald Maclean, and Maclean's later biographer and fellow diplomat, Robert Cecil, both felt that he had difficulties fitting in. Nonetheless, he did well and, despite his opposition to appeasement – shared by many in the Foreign Office – he ended up in the Central Department, the section that looked after relations with Nazi Germany. His intelligence would have been of vital interest to the NKVD, and what is interesting is that his ultimate superior there was Sir William Strang (later Lord Strang), who was educated at a state school in Essex and went to the University of London, not Oxford or Cambridge, and who was thus from a social background very similar to Cairncross' own. As Strang went on to be made a Lord and Permanent Under Secretary (i.e. the Head) of the Foreign Office, perhaps the place was not as socially elitist or exclusive after all.

But as one of Cairncross' biographers put it, his 'touchy and graceless manners' soon proved an irritant and he was transferred to the Treasury, possibly with the blessing of his then NKVD link Theodor Maly, before the latter had to return to the USSR and face a firing squad. Either way, at the Treasury, in the august Whitehall department that controlled Britain's money, he was equally of use to his NKVD employers. And in 1940 he hit the jackpot, becoming private secretary to Lord Hankey, one of the most powerful men in Britain, the first ever Secretary to the Cabinet, and now, in semi-retirement, a minister in the Churchill wartime coalition government and privy to some of the most important secrets of the entire war.

For Lord Hankey was in ministerial charge of British scientific research, and at the heart of this project was what was to be called Tube Alloys, a British cover name for what we now know as the Manhattan Project, the atomic bomb. And while the sheer cost of the enterprise meant that it was eventually bound to be an American-funded programme, much of the early ground-breaking research was British, and it was with this, the beginning of atomic weapons research, that Hankey was pivotal.

And so too, therefore, was John Cairncross, his private secretary.

We now get into denial/rebuttal territory. People who want to disbelieve anything that MI5 says, for example, are happy to believe his own version (which was believed fully by his obituary writer who stated that he was 'largely inactive as an agent until after the Nazi attack on Russia in 1941'.) Thus, for such people, he was a much-maligned man who only wanted to serve his country. And since, according to this version, he did not help the NKVD until *after* the Nazi invasion of the USSR, he was not really a traitor either.

But two kinds of source say otherwise. Not only does declassified British material say that, when working for Hankey, Cairncross was one of the NKVD's top spies, but so do the archives of the KGB itself, as well as the memoirs of former KGB agents, including those of Yuri Modin, who was Cairncross' Soviet NKVD controller after the war until Cairncross' exposure as a spy in 1951. So three very different sources all combine to say that Cairncross was very much a spy from 1940 to 1941, when the USSR was allied to our deadly enemy Nazi Germany. And the latter is vitally important in assessing the full scope of Cairncross' treachery, since he was giving atomic bomb research material to the USSR who was at that time the Third Reich's Nazi-Soviet Pact ally.

In other words we can see why the Soviets regarded Cairncross so highly and why the KGB would put him second in importance only to Philby, and thus, interestingly, ahead of the better known spies Burgess, Maclean and Blunt.

In his memoirs Cairncross said that the documentation making him the joint secretary of the Scientific Advisory Committee was a clerical error. Some typo! Cairncross saw all of the key material on how to enrich uranium to create atomic weapons and passed it on to his very grateful NKVD controllers.

This means that when Klaus Fuchs and Alan Nunn May became involved in the actual creation of the Tube Alloys Manhattan Project and the building of the bomb itself, the USSR already knew all the background scientific and technical details, as provided by Cairncross.

Hankey also had a roving brief in investigating the wartime intelligence services, and one of the odder things found in the Soviet archives (as outlined in Nigel West's book *Triplex*) is Hankey's report on how to reorganise MI5 and MI6, translated into Russian (and in West's book translated back into Hankey's original English!). This too came from Cairncross, and shows that he had access to all kinds of the very highest grade material that he apparently passed on in box loads to his NKVD handlers, who were, naturally, immensely appreciative.

In 1941 his time with Hankey came to an end and, rather than join up and fight as a frontline soldier, he was successfully transferred to Bletchley Park, where the famous Enigma decrypts were being deciphered, known as Ultra.

The Soviets were never given the Ultra material directly. Not only had they been an ally of the Nazis between 1939 and 1941 but Stalin, despite having countless warnings from Britain about the launch of Barbarossa in 1941, and from his own spies such as Richard Sorge in Tokyo, ignored them altogether, with the result that when the actual invasion came in 1941 the Red army was in all the wrong places and hundreds of thousands of Soviet troops were killed or captured in the first weeks.

There is a very strong argument for saying that no invasion of Russia will ever work, and Hitler's experience was to prove no different from Napoleon's in 1812, and although some advance divisions of the Wehrmacht reached within a few miles of the Moscow suburbs in December 1941, the Soviet counter-attack that month, in effect, wiped out any hope that Hitler's blitzkrieg against the USSR would ever succeed. Many historians argue – I think entirely correctly – that Barbarossa was doomed from the start, and so the Soviets would eventually have been able to launch a successful retaliatory invasion that would end the war.

But the cost was to be colossal – *27 million Soviet deaths* from 1941 to 1945 (it was originally thought the cost was a still staggering twenty million but recent research has revised the figures upwards), most of these being civilians slaughtered by the Nazis, who regarded Slavs as lesser human beings, in the same category, in effect, as they placed the Jews; most of the six million who died in the Holocaust coming from what had been either Polish or Soviet territory. In what became, in 1991, the independent country of Belarus, *25 per cent of the entire pre-1941 population* were murdered by the Germans, the Wehrmacht committing atrocities on the same scale as the SS.

Three things sped up the Soviet victory. First was the total disregard by Stalin for the lives of his own troops – it never mattered how many million soldiers died in the counter-attacks on the Germans. Secondly, the USA gave massive supplies to the USSR, and that, coupled with the fact that the Soviets were successfully able to relocate many of their munitions factories out in the distant Urals and beyond, out of German range, meant that, within a short space of time, the Red Army was overwhelmingly out-producing the Wehrmacht in tanks, guns and all sorts of vital war-winning armaments and equipment.

And third, although the British never officially revealed their sources, the Red Army was able to make use of the extensive decrypts that Ultra provided so that, in many battles, the Soviet commanders, just like their British or American equivalents, knew exactly what the German deployments were and could act accordingly.

There were, in fact, three Cambridge NKVD spies passing on Enigma material – Philby, as we have seen, Leo Long, who we shall look at later, and John Cairncross. But only the last was actually working at Bletchley itself, and was able to pass on the unadulterated version to his Soviet controllers. (So sensitive was the Ultra secret that even other government departments in Britain got the filtered version, often designed to look as if the source was, say, a spy in the Wehrmacht, or some local agent – but never a decrypt.) And, in the Soviet case, Britain was also worried that there might be German penetration of the Red Army or NKVD, so that if the Soviets overtly knew the true source of the material, the Germans would discover it too and alter all their codes; the source of Ultra would immediately dry up.

But, in the case of John Cairncross, he was able to deliver to the NKVD the raw original decrypts, totally without alteration or spin, something that Churchill and precious few others in Britain were able to see, such was the total secrecy with which the Bletchley Park material was enveloped.

One author has worked out, from delving into the Soviet archives, that Cairncross gave the NKVD no fewer than 5,832 documents – and those are only the ones that remain in Moscow today, so he could have given them even more. This is an epic amount by any standard, and it must rank Cairncross as one of the most productive spies in history.

As we saw with the cases of Blunt and Philby, the Soviets were so paranoid that they could hardly believe their luck and, for a while, some in the NKVD wondered seriously whether or not their Cambridge spies were actually double agents. In fact it was Cairncross who arguably proved that they were, in reality, completely loyal agents of the NKVD and not a bluff to insinuate MI6 agents into the Soviet intelligence system.

His clinching materials were the decrypts of what was probably the most important single battle of the Second World War – known now as the Battle of Kursk. One now known to be the biggest tank battle in history.

The failure to capture Stalingrad in 1942 meant that the Germans were beaten so far as the conquest of the USSR was concerned – not only had they failed to capture Moscow in 1941, but their second-wave attack in 1942, aimed at sweeping south to capture the Soviet oil fields in the Caucasus, had now failed as well. The Battle of Kursk was the last desperate gambler's throw, to launch a counter-attack against the Red Army in order finally to resurrect any possible last hope of victory and keep the war going.

The sheer scale of Kursk completely dwarfs anything fought against the Germans by either the British or the

Americans, D-day included. Indeed, as we have seen elsewhere, 85 per cent of German forces were engaged on the *Eastern Front* against the Soviets, and only 15 per cent against the western allies. Thanks to historians such as Norman Davies, and BBC historians and filmmakers such as Laurence Rees, we are now slowly beginning to realise this in Britain and the USA, but it was the central fact of the war back then, as Stalin well knew.

While Marshal Zhukov and other key Soviet commanders would have had the heavily censored version of British Ultra from the United Kingdom, and of a kind that would in itself have been considerably helpful in planning the Red Army defences at Kursk and counter-attacks, the fact that through Cairncross they had the actual full-detail, original material – called 'flimsies' – was of incalculable benefit since they could know every very last minute detail of what their German opponents were planning in *Zitadelle*, called 'Operation Citadel' in English.

The battle itself raged from July to August 1943. But thanks to Cairncross the Soviets had the Germans' full battle plans as early as February, and so had months to prepare. The sheer scale of Citadel/Kursk is overwhelming – well over *two million* soldiers, many in tanks, took part over the weeks of the fighting, and well over *one million were killed*, which is more killed in a single engagement on the Eastern Front than all the casualties of Britain and the USA combined, throughout the entire war. My wife's family was involved in the battle of the Bulge, which was a major battle of the western front, but compared to Citadel/Kursk even that was a minor skirmish, with Britain's greatest victory at El Alamein even more of a minnow compared to a whale.

And with all this, the information supplied officially by the British government and unofficially by John Cairncross played a pivotal role in giving the Soviets unbelievable and wholly accurate advance intelligence.

The NKVD was so profoundly grateful to Cairncross that he was given the very rare Soviet decoration of the Order of the Red Banner. Though, of course, he could only look at it when shown the medal by his controller, as it was hardly something he could have kept and taken home!

The Battle of Kursk has, in effect, acted as Cairncross' 'get out of jail free' card for being a traitor – it is not without coincidence that the espionage to which he admits fully in his memoirs is his major contribution to Kursk, and it is not without coincidence that his autobiography is called *The Enigma Spy*. For his argument is that, as the Soviets and British were allied in 1943 and, as it was vital to help our Russian allies as much as possible, what he did in giving over 5,000 decrypts (or flimsies) to the NKVD was not treason but actually helping an ally in time of greatest need. For example, thanks to him, the Red Army knew the entire disposition of the Luftwaffe before the battle itself, of inestimable value to the Soviet leadership.

But the British caveat – of the Soviets being penetrated by the Abwehr (German intelligence) – could have been true and Cairncross was taking a huge risk. And Kursk does not really get anyone out of jail. It does not bear thinking about that, if Bletchley was so lax in security that a Soviet spy could give over 5,000 documents away, a German spy could have done the same, with devastating consequences.

And because Cairncross helped with Kursk, it does not excuse his treachery both before his time in Bletchley and afterwards, especially his betrayal of the atomic bomb research, which, as we have seen, puts most of what Philby provided for them into the shade.

Unlike Philby, Cairncross, like Blunt, found being a spy and the double life it involved enormously stressful – he was not a natural secret agent. Indeed, if one reads the account of one of his Soviet controllers, Yuri Modin, in *My Five Cambridge Friends*, one gets two very strong impressions: that of an agent of spectacular usefulness and equally spectacular clumsiness and total lack of what John le Carré fans would now call tradecraft. In fact, a better modern analogy would be Mr Bean, since Cairncross' personality and his lack of *savoir faire* must have made him a nightmare agent to have run.

His glory days – working for Hankey and then for Bletchley Park – ended the same year as the battle of Kursk, 1943. He was transferred to MI6 itself (known more properly then, as now, as SIS) and was in a part of MI6 responsible for the security of overseas counter-espionage.

The irony of this, as with Kim Philby in a closely related form of work in MI6, is total – an NKVD spy working to prevent spies from messing up the work overseas of British intelligence... How much he knew about Kim Philby is something we will probably never know, even though Philby was instrumental in recruiting those who recruited him, and both of them were at Trinity, albeit at not exactly the same time span. When Philby wrote his memoirs he would not have known that Cairncross had long since confessed, unlike the much-exposed Burgess and Maclean, so the former naturally does not appear in *My Secret War*. And as *The Enigma Spy* has been shown to be equally unreliable in downplaying its author's role, we cannot gauge from either book how knowingly the two men collaborated in 1943 to 1945.

MI6 did not keep all its wartime recruits – which, in view of how many of them were actually working for the NKVD is probably just as well – and Cairncross was among those who left. He went back to the Treasury, in which he served (with a time of secondment to the Ministry of Supply) until his exposure in 1951.

Here again his recollections are faulty or deliberately misleading. He claimed to have given up being a spy. But as with many things, this too is false, since he was now in an excellent position to give very valuable information to the NKVD/KGB. Here his knowledge, as now exposed by both British and Soviet sources in equal abundance, was of great value to the USSR, although never again on the same scale as his information on the early atom bomb research or on Kursk.

However, as Defence Material was part of his brief at both ministries, he was able to give considerable volumes of documentation to Yuri Modin, now his NKVD controller, on the finances of the atom bomb. The details of this, including the crucial scientific data, was now coming from Klaus Fuchs who was working on the actual project itself, and, as we saw, from Donald Maclean in Washington DC. But the Soviets were delighted with the financial secrets he was giving them and, as Modin recalled years later: 'I liked Cairncross best of all our London agents. He wasn't an easy man to deal with, but he was a profoundly decent one'.

Similarly, when NATO was formed, massive amounts of new British Government funding was necessary. Because of his job, Cairncross gave the KGB (as it was soon called) information on every possible aspect of all the finance the NATO allies required. He was also able to provide intricate details on British defence spending and, in particular, the plans of what Britain would do in the event of war with the USSR and what was to become the Warsaw Pact (later on in the 1950s, but under increasing Soviet control even earlier).

According to Modin, Cairncross was completely absent-minded about their secret assignations, sometimes forgetting to turn up at all, or coming to the wrong place or to the right place at the wrong time. (Once more Mr Bean comes strongly to mind.) He was so terrible a photographer that he had to take the documents out of the Treasury (itself a huge risk) and have them photographed by the KGB before they could be returned to the safe. At one stage both Modin and Cairncross were stopped in a car by the police – Cairncross was a catastrophic driver as well – and, as Modin recalls, it was just as well that no identity papers were called for or that the car was not searched, as the Modin/Cairncross spy network would have been ended there and then. (And since Modin was also Burgess' controller, the ramifications would have been wider still...)

So, of Cairncross' continuing treachery, there can be no doubt.

But then, when Burgess fled in 1951, some incriminating material was left in his apartment, despite Blunt doing his best to get rid of anything that would lead to any of the other Cambridge spies. This was a briefing document from 1939, written by Cairncross for the use of Burgess, and unfortunately for Cairncross, Jock Colville, who had been at Trinity and the Foreign Office with him, recognised the handwriting.

In all but name this was the end of Cairncross' career as a spy. Since there was precious little evidence against him – he had managed to avoid a meeting with Modin at which both men would certainly have been caught – he agreed to tell MI5 that he had passed things occasionally to the Soviets but that he had never been an NKVD spy.

This was nonsense but, since British intelligence was in a state of complete shock after the Burgess/Maclean defection, all the other major Cambridge spies were able to get away with it in 1951, as we have noticed already with both Philby and Blunt.

For Cairncross 1951 to 1952, therefore, meant a whole new life. At the same time as his exposure he had got married, to a German Jewish refugee called Gabriele Oppenheim, whom, he claimed, never knew of his treachery (and in this instance it is always possible that he is telling the truth). This marriage did not last more than a decade in practice, although he waited until her death in 1995 to marry his long-time friend Gayle, an American opera singer many years his junior and who has very strongly defended him and his innocence of anything more than passing on the secrets of Kursk to the Russians.

(He also wrote a book entitled *After Polygamy Was Made a Sin*, which his wartime friend and SIS former colleague Graham Greene, the novelist, commented in reviewing it that the work was good news for polygamists! The extent to which Cairncross practised what he preached is naturally open to conjecture.)

Most of his life was consequently spent abroad. He spent time as an accredited correspondent in Rome, worked for three years for the United Nations in Geneva and then for five years was employed in Bangkok as a senior editor for the Economic Council for Asia and what was then called the Far East (now East Asia). He spent one year in Pakistan, giving advice to that country, in conjunction with Harvard University, on how to plan the economy.

Then in 1963 he applied for a job that he really wanted – at what was then called Western Reserve University (now called Case Western Reserve University), a distinguished university in Cleveland, Ohio. Happiness at last!

But now his past caught up with him. He had continued to be interviewed over the years by MI5, most notably by Arthur Martin and also by someone who was much later to become notorious: Peter Wright. Wright is now infamous as the author of *Spycatcher,* the book that the British government tried unsuccessfully to ban in Australia, and which was filled with all kinds of paranoia – spies everywhere – of the kind that James Jesus Angleton made equally odious in the USA at the same period.

In 1964, as we know, Blunt decided to confess everything, having been exposed by Michael Straight. This in turn heavily implicated Cairncross, his former pupil at Trinity.

Consequently Cairncross had to confess all, a move which also ruined his ability to stay at Western Reserve as the FBI were, understandably, not keen to have an ex-NKVD agent on their soil. He thought that he had an immunity deal similar to the one enjoyed by Blunt and, while that might have been the case, nonetheless the Security Service was not able to protect him against discovery by nosy journalists trying to discover the truth.

For, in effect, when Philby, the Third Man, fled in 1963 (one presumes this was another reason for the pressure on Cairncross and Blunt to confess), the hunt was on for other spies, known, ever since *Tinker, Tailor, Soldier, Spy* and sequential novels as *moles*.

Cairncross was able to live under the radar in Europe for many years, with occasional chats with Peter Wright (who like Angleton was seeking non-existent moles) and with a tacit understanding that he could only come back to Britain with the consent of MI5, which he was, very occasionally, allowed to do.

As Stella Rimington, the first ever female head of MI5 (the first of two to hold the post) later said, when she interrogated him in the 1970s over old ground, he was: 'determined to... tell us no more than he had already admitted, which was nothing like the full story'. Since his memoirs are filled with bile against MI5 from failing to protect him in the years after this, one can rather see why they felt that to hide him from the consequences of his earlier treachery was not exactly a high priority for them, especially if there really were major secrets which, as the future Dame Stella correctly guessed, he was continuing to hide from them long after the events.

Then, in 1979, came the exposure of Anthony Blunt, the Fourth Man. Everyone was soon looking for a Fifth Man – it was already known that the USSR had employed a 'ring of five' Cambridge graduates back in the 1930s – and so the likely suspect could be one of a very small number of people. After Blunt's outing some wholly innocent

Cambridge alumni were suspected wrongly of being the fifth member of the group, but it soon became more than apparent to anyone who did some serious research that Cairncross was the person in question. In particular, three very able journalists, Barry Penrose, David Leitch and Simon Freeman, discovered the truth, exposing Cairncross in the *Sunday Times* and later in the Penrose/Freeman book *Conspiracy of Silence*. The cat was out of the proverbial bag.

Cairncross was incandescent at being outed as a spy and was venomous to MI5 for, as he felt, hanging him out to dry. As with Blunt he refused to tell things to journalists and television on the basis that everything was covered in silence under the Official Secrets Act. The irony of two former NKVD agents invoking this act was, of course, not lost on the angry media and watching world.

In 1982 he was found guilty – but not of espionage. He was convicted for currency smuggling, across the Swiss-Italian border. In 1990, by which time he was trying to live a low-key lotus-eating life in the south of France, he once again burst into publicity. By now Oleg Gordievsky had defected to Britain and, in conjunction with Professor Christopher Andrew of the University of Cambridge, written a book entitled *KGB: The Inside Story* which, with Gordievsky's evidence to hand, once again exposed Cairncross as the Fifth Man, and this time with the revelation of his full treachery, including his betrayal of the early atomic bomb secrets in 1940 to 1941. Cairncross was not merely the Fifth Man, but *an important spy*.

(David Leitch, who exposed Cairncross after Blunt, was to write the preface to Modin's book *My Five Cambridge*

Friends. As he put it there, it vindicated completely the idea that Cairncross had been very much one of the Cambridge Five and as important as Philby – the Andrew/Gordievsky book that so upset Cairncross was therefore also entirely vindicated by Modin's memoirs and by the research that Leitch, Freeman and Penrose had initiated.)

Despite all this, and perhaps because he was now old and frail, he was allowed by MI5 to come back to live in Britain. He died on 8 October 1995, near Leominster, in the west of England, exposed fully as the traitor he had been, but never prosecuted.

He thought of himself as the Enigma Spy. David Leitch has likened him to a character from the famous 1940s Ealing Comedies (and for us he is Mr Bean as secret agent). But, in reality, he was one of the major atomic bomb spies, and that is why I have put him in this chapter, along with the other Cambridge atomic spy, Alan Nunn May, to whom we can now turn.

He was born in a suburb of Birmingham on 2nd May 1911, the son of middle-class parents. He attended King Edward VI Foundation school there – a famous sixteenth century foundation for the clever but not socially privileged, and was then fortunate to gain a scholarship to Trinity Hall, with which we are familiar through the career of his contemporary there Donald Maclean.

And both Nunn May and Maclean were friends, although one was in the sciences and the other in the humanities. How much did they know of each other's communist views? According to what we seem to know about Nunn May, it was not until 1942 that he began actively to spy for the NKVD, when his work became useful to the USSR. But had he and

Maclean ever discussed such things earlier? Sadly we do not know.

As an undergraduate the fellow keeping an eye on his welfare was Patrick Blackett. Blackett was a strong socialist and, like many intellectuals of the time, took a very sympathetic view of the USSR, especially as the Soviet Union was also seen (pre-August 1939) as the bulwark against the growing fascist menace.

But Blackett was no traitor and was, indeed, a patriot, one of those most involved during the Second World War in what is called operational research, the application of science to military use, which in his case proved invaluable to the scientific fight against Nazi Germany. When it came to atomic weapons research it was Blackett's view that prevailed – some wanted Britain to have its own atomic bomb during the war, whereas Blackett realised that only in collaboration with the USA could proper development have a chance of coming to fruition. He was vindicated – the Manhattan Project was a US-UK joint effort.

(He was very dubious, though, after the war on whether or not such weapons could 'win' a war for either side – he tended to think that neutral use of the bomb was better than cold war, as he expressed in his work published in the USA as *Fear, War and the Bomb*.)

But his path was very different from Nunn May's. He continued a distinguished scientific career, working with governments of all political stripes (while remaining himself close to the Labour Party), and ended up as President of the Royal Society from 1965 to 1970 and as Lord Blackett. And, as for his ultimate political loyalties, he was cleared throughout his career for very confidential work, his patriotism unquestioned. So socialism in the 1930s and sympathy for a kinder attitude to the USSR, as evinced by Blackett's life, show that treason of a kind that his pupil Alan Nunn May was about to begin was an exception not a rule.

Nunn May also took a PhD in physics. His initial war-related work was on radar, but by 1942 he found himself involved in the early days of Tube Alloys, the Manhattan Project that was to create the first atomic bombs.

One of his discoveries that year was about the German attempts to create a weapon of mass destruction – what he, in later years, would confess as being a 'dirty bomb'. Although since what we now call a dirty bomb is a different kind of beast, one that creates intense radioactive material over a small area as opposed to an atomic weapon that spreads it over a wide area, one wonders what exactly it was that he was reading, or whether the nomenclature has changed.

Whatever the case he became concerned that such a bomb could be used against the Soviet Union, and so he got in touch with someone he knew in Soviet intelligence – how interesting that he knew whom to contact – and told them of his worries.

And, in January 1943, that new relationship with the Soviets proved to be a bonus as his team, which had been based back in Cambridge itself, was transferred *en bloc* to Montreal in Canada. Here, he and his colleagues were tasked with putting together a 'heavy water' reactor, which would, in turn, be set up at Chalk River, in Ontario.

Unlike the top Soviet atom bomb spy, Klaus Fuchs, Nunn May was therefore not actually in the Manhattan Project itself, the holy of holies of atomic weapons research. But the Canada-based team worked very closely with their colleagues in the USA, and what one group knew so did the other, to their mutual benefit and, of course, to that of the USSR, since it was Beria, the head of the NKVD, who was also in charge of Soviet atomic weapons development.

Alan Nunn May always insisted that in 1943 to 1945 he did not spy for the Soviets while based in Montreal, and it was not until he was approached again by Russian military intelligence (the GRU) in early 1945 that he resumed his treacherous career. This might, of course, be possible but, as with all who betray their country, how can one tell whether or not it was true?

Either way, at the beginning of 1945, the GRU contacted Nunn May in his house in Montreal, with an eager plea for help. Lieutenant Pavel Angelov of the GRU had been assigned to look after Nunn May in 1945, and now he came to see him to ask for samples of uranium of the kind that was to be used in the atomic bomb the British and Americans were about to test.

(The Soviets had, of course, known all about such research for years – in part, as we have now seen, thanks to John Cairncross, with Nunn May's Trinity Hall contemporary Donald Maclean soon getting a pivotal role in finding out progress through his job in Washington DC.)

Some have argued that Nunn May was hesitant at giving them such high grade material – he knew the depth of the treason that he was about to commit. At this distance it is hard to tell either way. But, reluctantly or not, he now gave them the crown jewels. Not merely did he write two astonishingly in-depth reports on scientific progress and on the entire structure of the Manhattan Project itself – both these things being possible since, as part of his research in Canada, he had been able to go to Chicago in the USA, not too far away, and discover all kinds of invaluable material at the Argonne National Laboratory that was based there. Indeed, as he later confessed, he was allowed to look at virtually anything he wanted, hand them to his Soviet controllers who copied them, and then hand the secrets back again, all without being suspected at all by the Americans – let alone the British or Canadians.

He was also able to give them microscopic samples of the two key uranium isotopes essential to making the bomb – U233 and U235, on a strip of platinum foil. This was an especial boost for the GRU, since their other agent there had said that to hand over such critical material would be impossible: Nunn May proved them wrong. It is not surprising that the Soviets were delirious with this good news and gave their GRU staff medals as a reward.

In September 1945 he went back to Britain, where he intended to resume his pre-war career as a lecturer at the University of London. All might have been well but for a piece of bad luck for him and good fortune for the British and Americans – Igor Gouzenko, a cipher clerk at the Soviet embassy in Ottowa, who was afraid of going home to the USSR, decided that the brave thing to do would be to escape and come over to the British and Canadians. And Gouzenko had information – the GRU had a spy in atomic weapons research in Canada...

Now we come back to a question I asked earlier about conspiracy theories. Is a glass half full or half empty? We now have the official histories of MI5 (and of MI6 but only up to 1949). Half empty: there must be much we still *don't know* and that 'they' are hiding from us. Half full: but at least we know *something* and to know even a small amount of hitherto top secret material is much better than knowing none of it at all, especially as so much of the speculation in the past has been such rubbish.

And so with Alan Nunn May, as with all the other spies we are considering in this book, there is much that is still unknown, though his deathbed confession to his family, even though perhaps misleading, does tell us a few things.

But, thanks to the official histories, we know a whole lot more than the people who wrote back in the 1950s about the atom bomb spies (mainly about Klaus Fuchs, but about Alan Nunn May as well). For example, they did not know then that Kim Philby was a Soviet agent and, therefore, that Philby played a major role in trying to get Nunn May to escape or to avoid prosecution. Philby himself, as we saw, wrote memoirs that were unfortunately mendacious, so would not tell us the truth at all. But we now know many things about how MI5 tried to capture Alan Nunn May as soon as Gousenko defected to Canada, and how Philby did his best to stop them – remember, he himself was not under any suspicion until 1951 and, even then, many believed him innocent until his own defection in 1963.

It became very obvious from Gousenko that the GRU spy in Canada could only be one man, and that was Alan Nunn May. But, in Britain, rules of evidence are enormously strict and evidence from a Soviet defector could not, certainly at that time, be used in a British court. So Nunn May could not be prosecuted successfully on Gousenko's evidence, especially since Gousenko did not actually know Nunn May's real name, only his Soviet codename.

The idea then arose that the best thing to do would be to catch Nunn May, now back in London, *in flagrante* – passing on secrets to his new London-based GRU controller. (As we saw earlier in this chapter, that almost happened with Cairncross and Modin, had the policeman who stopped them been more inquisitive.)

But remember who at MI6 was in charge of anti-Soviet counter-intelligence: Kim Philby.

So, although the main responsibility for catching Nunn May was with MI5, who in any case were the main link with Canada instead of MI6 because Canada was part of the soon-to-be-named Commonwealth, Philby intervened as much as possible, eager to limit any damage to his NKVD colleagues that Gousenko could inflict, especially if Gousenko (a GRU officer) might implicate *him*.

There is no doubt, therefore, that when Nunn May was supposed to meet his GRU controller at a pre-arranged meeting at the British Museum, Philby tipped him off and aborted the rendezvous.

And, in fact, as we now know Philby told the NKVD that he ensured that Nunn May did not 'put a foot wrong' since getting back to Britain, and that this therefore was of huge frustration to MI5, since he was carefully not doing anything to incriminate himself. In turn the NKVD would have informed the GRU to tell Nunn May that he was under suspicion, thereby thwarting the prosecution case.

Thankfully for MI5, Nunn May turned out not to be the 'tough customer' they presumed him to be. He was now working on atomic research at the large Harwell Laboratory that still exists just outside Oxford. There he was cross-questioned, not by MI5 but by Commander Lionel Burt, of Scotland Yard, on 15th February 1946 – the delay being caused by the need to wait until Gousenko's defection in Canada could be made public.

It seems that, while admitting nothing, Nunn May went as white as a sheet and, to the experienced eye of his police interrogator, looked distinctly guilty. Four days later Burt had another go at him and, by making the case against him look much stronger than it really was (remember that all MI5 and the police had was Gousenko's inadmissible evidence), caused Nunn May to crack.

With Nunn May's confession a trial could take place and he was duly sentenced to ten years' penal servitude after just a single day.

Nunn May was therefore the only Cambridge spy to go to jail – all the others either defected or were able to gain immunity deals in return for giving evidence. And an interesting contrast: in the USA, similar spies, such as the Krogers, were executed for treason. Nunn May was a traitor but it was prison rather than the gallows that confronted him. In fact, many left-wing intellectuals thought that even ten years was too much and he was fortunate to be let out after serving just six and a half.

He went back to Cambridge on release in 1953, and he married an Austrian lady who, because he had already been in jail, knew of his treasonous past. He was not able to get any further university posts, but was able to work for a scientific instruments company until, in 1961, JD Bernal, a well-known academic (and strong left-wing sympathiser) was able to get him a major job in Ghana, a newly independent African country whose dictator, Nkrumah, had no problems with pro-Soviet thinkers gaining university posts. So, for seventeen years, from 1961 to 1978, Nunn May was a professor (and, for a while, also Dean) of the new University of Ghana, ending his days as a scientific adviser to the Ghanaian government.

By 1978 any treason he had committed was long in the past. He was allowed to come back to live quietly in Cambridge, and in 2002, when he was very ill, he gave his step-granddaughter a confession of his espionage, insisting in doing so that he had done nothing wrong. On 12th January 2003 he died in Cambridge, rather appropriately in the university city where his spying career had begun.

As his biographer Brian Cathcart is right to say, Nunn May did not give anything like as much information to the Soviets as Klaus Fuchs, who was uncovered in the 1950s, also jailed but, in his case, allowed to emigrate to the then East Germany (the DDR). But, as Cathcart also correctly concludes, the very existence of atom bomb spies did huge damage to the US-UK atomic research relationship, leading directly to the McMahon Act of the US Congress, which expressly forbade British-American collaboration.

The fact that Britain then had to spend millions on its own nuclear weapons research stems from this, and one could therefore argue that Nunn May's treachery led to Trident, since otherwise the British could have continued to rely on the American nuclear shield and not bothered to have an exceedingly expensive nuclear armaments programme of their own. Considering the billions Britain has spent on its own deterrent capability, one could say that Nunn May is the costliest spy in history.

THE LONG AND THE STRAIGHT

Leo Long & Michael Straight

So Anthony Blunt was the Fourth Man and John Cairncross the Fifth Man. But how does one go on counting? Alan Nunn May, who is never given a number, was, in fact, the first Cambridge spy from the 1930s to be exposed, and he was a friend at Trinity Hall of Donald Maclean, who, since Burgess usually goes first for alphabetic reasons, must presumably be described as the Second Man.

What number, therefore, are the two we will look at in this chapter – Leo Long and Michael Straight? Both have education at Trinity College in common (along with Philby, Blunt and Burgess), and were, according to Blunt's confession in 1964, recruited by him personally before the war.

(The famous novelist Alexander McCall Smith has written a humorous short story called *The Sixth or Seventh Man*, set in Scotland and free of any links with the University of Cambridge. It is enormous fun and was reproduced in the New Statesman in 2012. But sadly it is irrelevant to our tale, except that Straight or Long could each easily be called the Sixth or Seventh Man.)

Both of these spies show how dangerous it is to believe in caricatures. The Apostles was not a society primarily of aesthetes, although it contained many, as we saw in the chapter on Blunt. And since both Long and Straight became Apostles, from very different social backgrounds and both were heterosexual, their very presence in that group shows that we cannot put everyone into the same box.

This is especially true of Leo Long, who came from a working-class family in North London (from Holloway). His father was a carpenter who was often out of work and, in the 1930s, before the advent of the welfare state after the war, the consequences of that could be dire. In fact, as he reflected years later, his scholarship (in Modern Languages, to Trinity) was worth £250 a year in the money of that time and that, in a good year with plenty of work, his father's average income was less than half that, or around £110 a year. This was very far away indeed from the privileged lifestyles of the normal young undergraduate at Cambridge at the time, including of those who were, like Long, to go on to spy for the USSR.

In fact we know very little of Leo Long at all – including the year of his birth and that of his death. He is certainly one of the Cambridge spy ring, the Sixth or Seventh Man, and his links with Blunt in particular lasted some while. But, while he was found very much alive when exposed as a spy by Barry Penrose and Simon Freeman when they wrote their life of Blunt, *Conspiracy of Silence* in 1986, he does not otherwise appear. Much of what we do know of him is thanks to Penrose and Freeman and their interviews with him, since he does not appear much in the authorised history of MI5.

And, interestingly, Trinity College is one of the few colleges that does not have much information on its post-1900 alumni in the Cambridge University Library, although King's College, the other main supplier of members of the Apostles, has details right up to the present day.

Therefore we have to hope that what Long recalled, many years after the events he was describing, is accurate.

And perhaps his greatest importance is not what he did when he spied for the NKVD but his codename, ELLI.

This may now seem arcane but, for decades, it was the source of virtual civil war within MI5, and led to all kinds of entirely innocent people, including a Director of the Service, Sir Roger Hollis, being accused falsely of treachery. This is because, for years, it was thought that ELLI, clearly the codename for a British agent for the NKVD, was none other than Sir Roger himself, despite the paucity of evidence to prove this. (And there are still old warriors who insist, aeons after the events, that they are right; now seen as more than unlikely.)

However, when Oleg Gordievsky came over to Britain in the 1980s, he was able to solve one of the oldest mysteries in British intelligence, going back nearly four decades to the first decrypts of the Soviet VENONA material. ELLI was indeed a British NKVD agent – but he was *Leo Long*, and not the blameless Sir Roger Hollis. And, as we shall see, by this time the British had long since known of Long's treachery during the Second World War and afterwards, and had even given him legal immunity from prosecution since, as we saw, SIGINT (Signals Intelligence) could not be used as evidence in British courts, even though the USSR had, for ages, known of the VENONA material because of Kim Philby's treachery. As Christopher Andrew rightly says, huge amounts of time and effort would have been spared if only MI5 had known that they knew who ELLI was all along.

Long, therefore, like Cairncross, was from an atypical background for 1930s Cambridge, not being part of the elegant youth and world of privilege that predominated in those days. Indeed, it seems that he thought his environment a 'strange world... an extension, for most people, of life at public school'.

But, as many have pointed out, Long was nowhere near as awkward or ill at ease as Cairncross and, in any case, while he did not find many working-class people at Cambridge, he did find plenty of fellow Marxists, and soon found much ideological companionship there.

Among such fellow travellers he soon found himself in the company of Blunt and Burgess – Blunt taught him French – and of the most illustrious young communist of their day, John Cornford. Cornford will come up again in this chapter. We have already seen him as the heroic young man who went to Spain to fight fascists and who became a legendary martyr for the cause when he died there in battle.

Once again, the glamour of the Spanish civil war was a major recruiting tool for the Comintern, and Long was recruited to spy for the Soviets through Blunt. Long summarises the view of a whole generation: 'We did not trust the British government. It seemed to prefer links to the Nazis to having ties with Russia...'. Sadly this was not far off the mark – though, as we have seen, there is a vast difference between being a socialist, as many were in those heady, idealistic times, and being a spy.

Long was recruited for the Apostles, and this is interesting given his social background and orientation. Clearly not all the Apostles were what someone described as 'Bollinger Bolsheviks'! Significantly, Long was not over-impressed with the standards of debate either. Being raised in the real world, not in the rarefied atmosphere of play-acting private schoolboys, he knew that rather a lot of the discussion was fairly delusional: 'The Apostles weren't going to take over the world... It was a bit of a racket really. They weren't the brightest people at all...'. Thus does Long's North London realism puncture many of the myths of the Apostles as an all-powerful cabal.

As we saw, most of the Cambridge spies were recruited on the grounds of their long-term promise, rather than because they already occupied secret positions from which they could pass on top grade material to their Soviet spymasters.

So Long initially went to Germany to teach, having to return to Britain when the war broke out and joining an elite regiment, the Oxford and Buckinghamshire Light Infantry – later part of the even more elite Royal Green Jackets (and now, in recent reshuffles, part of The Rifles). But, being a Cambridge languages graduate, he was naturally asked to sign up for intelligence and, in December 1940, this is what he proceeded to do. As he recalled years later, no one asked him about his political views and, in any case, since Nazi Germany was the main enemy, hints of youthful communism would, at this stage, not have counted against him any more than it did those many graduates from the 1930s for whom socialism was the only possible bulwark against the fascist threat.

He found himself in MI14. This was established to find out as much as possible about Germany – Long's speaking German would have been of huge help – and it played a vital, albeit now-forgotten and unsung, role during the war. Its intelligence information was essential for the army chiefs, since MI14, along with other kinds of intelligence gained from MI6, SOE and Bletchley Park, told them all they needed to know about the size of the German forces, right down to unit level.

Long later recalled that this was around-the-clock work, with sixteen-hour days and often six days a week, so important was what he was doing.

And it was at precisely so hectic a time that Blunt appeared, now, as we saw, officially working for MI5 but also, and principally, for the Soviet Union as well, almost immediately after the launch of Barbarossa in June 1941.

Like all the other Cambridge spies, Long does not seem to have been fazed by the Molotov-Ribbentrop Pact between the Soviets and Nazis in August 1939, unlike many other graduates of Oxford and Cambridge, whose flirtation with communism ended when they saw Stalin betray the anti-fascist popular front against the dictators.

As with Cairncross, Blunt felt that the British government was cheating the USSR of key data, just in order to survive. (Remember, at the time many in the west doubted that the Soviet Union could survive – it is really only in retrospect that the sheer impossibility of being able to conquer so vast a country has become obvious to historians.) He therefore wanted Long to give him as much material as possible, that he in turn would pass on to the Soviets.

Long later professed to have been queasy about Blunt's request, though whether or not that is later self-justification is hard to know. It certainly did not stop him at the time because, for the next three years, Blunt and Long would establish a regular weekly routine, with Long handing over to Blunt anything useful that he had obtained that week – and sometimes that was a considerably large amount of material.

Most espionage historians have commented that the NKVD loved gossip being passed on as much as hard data, though, in reality, how this could have been of real use is dubious, unless, as in the case of Philby, gossip was power. But to Long, who had no intention of staying in such exhausting work after the war, all this was completely boring, and he declined to pass on insider information of the kind that Blunt's Soviet controller wanted.

He did, however, pass on the results of Ultra intelligence from Bletchley, to which he was able to have access – and here again his insistence, years later, that he never actually passed on intercepts has to be taken with caution.

And, as time went by, he began to find his double life rather stressful. Ironically since, while he thought that Blunt was a cool customer always firmly in charge of his own emotions, we know now that Blunt himself was under perpetual emotional and psychological strain for exactly the same reasons.

By 1944 Long wanted out. He transferred to Field Marshal Montgomery's 21st Army Group, which was now embarking on the invasion of Europe, and would fight all the way from D-Day in Normandy to VE Day on the north German plain in 1945. Long was aware that he had committed treason and one of his contemporaries, Noel Annan (later Lord Annan and Provost of King's College, Cambridge), who worked with Long in MI14 and who knew many of the Cambridge spy ring, has commented that Long and Blunt were both as arrogant as each other, and had Long's material been captured by the Germans in Russia, then huge damage could have been done to the war effort.

And, as many historians have commented, Long's work was also important in that it gave invaluable corroboration to the Soviets of the material that Cairncross was providing from Bletchley Park.

Long then vanishes from view, until he turns up again in the trip that we read about in the chapter on Blunt, when the latter went to Germany to fetch manuscripts from various of King George VI's German relatives. This trip was to create all kinds of speculation on what exactly was in the material that Blunt was fetching.

Leo Long, by then, was back in civilian life but working for the British Occupation Zone, in the intelligence branch of the British Control Commission. This ruled part of Germany with the other allies until independence was permitted in 1949 (when Germany split into the larger pro-western part and the smaller communist-controlled German Democratic Republic, or DDR).

There has been much discussion on whether or not Long was a spy during this period. Since the Soviets controlled much of Germany, knowledge of what was happening in the British, American and French zones would have been most useful. He would also have known about the spies that the west was trying to infiltrate into the Soviet zone.

So was he a spy? He denied it when asked by Penrose and Freeman in the 1980s but, as the saying goes: he would say that, wouldn't he...? He certainly helped Blunt during the latter's royal mission and when, in 1946, his time in Germany seemed to be coming to a natural end, he requested to join either MI5 or MI6 on a permanent basis. And the person who gave him a reference as suitable for such intelligence work was no less than Blunt.

However, Sir Dick White, who was uniquely to serve as Head of both MI5 and of MI6, thought otherwise, and recommended him to try a university career instead. White maintained later that he had no suspicions of Long at the time, and was deeply appalled when he heard how closely Blunt and Long had been working for the Soviets.

In recollection, Long later denied that he and Blunt had continued as Soviet spies. But we now understand from the Soviet archives that in 1946, the year that Blunt recommended Long to MI5 or MI6, Blunt passed to his Soviet controller extensive material on the intelligence structure in the British zone of Germany. Either Long's memory is faulty or he is being what has been described in a related context as 'economical with the truth'.

And that is the last we hear of Leo Long for some years to come! He got married and started a family which knew nothing of his espionage activities, including the parts that were wholly patriotic, since the existence of Bletchley Park, although well known to the Soviets through Philby and Cairncross, was kept secret from the British public until the late 1960s. Even seventy years later many ex-Bletchley people still prefer not even to mention their experiences there.

But, in 1964, thanks to the other person we are looking at in this chapter, the American Michael Straight, Blunt was finally forced to confess. When he did so he was careful not to give too much away – as MI5's Arthur Martin noted ruefully – but he did let the security interrogators know that he had recruited Leo Long as a spy.

Long had spent an unobtrusive life living in Hampstead, a part of North London not far away from his childhood home of Holloway, but much more upper-middle class and respectable. He had worked both in the City of London and then in the film industry. Until then he had presumed that his double life had been unnoticed, but a phone call from Anthony Blunt summoning him to the latter's flat in the Courtauld made him realise that, eighteen years after he left the world of intelligence, his past had finally caught up with him.

Both Long and Blunt were interrogated by Arthur Martin. Long discovered, to his intense relief that, as his espionage was old history rather than current, it was unlikely that he would be prosecuted – and it would have been unfair if Blunt had been offered immunity for information and he had not. It is interesting to get Martin's own view, however, which was that Long seemed shocked and craven.

For the time being Long was off the hook, but not permanently, as others from MI5 would come in, over the years, to interrogate him further. He insisted that there was no more that he could say, and that all his actions could be explained by the hatred that many who loathed Nazism felt at the time. But, unlike him, many pre-war communists had been appalled by Stalin and realised the truth, so never betrayed their country.

Then, in 1979, Blunt was exposed and eager journalists started to ask questions. Blunt himself did not give Long's name away to the public, but Michael Straight did, to Penrose and Freeman two years later in 1981.

From their time with Long comes much of the information in this chapter, and indeed on Long himself in general, since he has not been written about much elsewhere. Now his treachery became public, with an interview with Freeman and his photograph in the *Sunday Times*. And, for a while, he even contemplated suicide – he was relieved that his past was now in the open, but he had been obliged to tell his wife.

And there Long vanishes from our view – a search of the internet does not bring an obituary but, were he alive, he would by now be a centenarian, so it is unlikely that he is still alive and more probable that he has gone to meet Marx. Perhaps he was not the most important of the Cambridge spies, but he certainly was of their number and, in his own way, as much a traitor as they were, even if, like Blunt, he found it all a bit much and retired from the fray.

With the other spy in our chapter, Michael Straight, we are at one moment on firmer ground – we have his full biographical details, from birth to death – but still on controversial territory, since it is a matter of much dispute as to how much of a spy he was at all. Since the overwhelming part of his life was spent in his native USA, he does not appear much in British archival sources, and thus is not much more than a cameo in the official histories.

Much, therefore, of what is known of him is through interview, and also conjecture, and this is where we enter murky waters.

For the best in-depth treatment of Straight is by an author who feels that Victor (later Lord) Rothschild was also a Soviet agent, a view for which he is in a minority of those writing on the subject – and for which there is no archival evidence. According to this view, Straight was working for the KGB right through until the end, and was an agent, therefore, of much greater importance than anyone had realised. But much of the proof offered is also anecdotal, and that is the same for that author's treatment of Victor Rothschild.

We will look in more detail on Rothschild when we ask if there were indeed other Cambridge spies who have slipped wider attention. With Straight there is plenty of incontrovertible evidence for an earlier part of his life, especially that at Cambridge, and it is only for his subsequent life, about which he wrote in his apologia, *After Long Silence*, that doubt on either side begins to creep in to what really happened and when.

Straight was born on 1st September 1916, into a branch of one of the wealthiest families in the USA. His father, Willard Straight (who died while Michael was still young), was wealthy enough as a successful diplomat. But his mother was Dorothy Payne Whitney, from the same family that founded the Whitney collection of American art in New York, and was one of the super-rich families of the Gilded Age. She later married the eccentric British founder of the progressive/experimental school Dartington Hall, Leonard Elmhirst, and so young Michael was born American but raised in his childhood in England. His brother Whitney Straight was to become British, and to be a co-founder of what later became British Airways.

Trinity College was thus an inevitable place for so privileged a youth, and Straight soon entered the social cliques that mattered, including that of Anthony Blunt. And, once again, we have a heterosexual Apostle, as he was naturally soon a member of that body as well, along with working-class Leo Long.

Like many young men of immense wealth and tender conscience, Straight felt guilty, in what we could call a perpetual state of acute angst. Being also British-American he felt uncertain of where exactly it was he belonged.

He was thus the ideal recruit for talent-spotters in Cambridge; in this case John Cornford and James Klugmann, names with which we are familiar already. Straight had spent an interim year at the London School of Economics, and his views there were already heading in a leftward direction.

So, consequently, his recruitment to the Communist Party in Cambridge was only a matter of time, especially since, by now, the communists could also portray themselves as one of the parties of the popular front against fascism, which included more respectable parties of the left, such as in France. His big hero was John Cornford who, as we recall, was to go to his death in Spain and thus always be the young heroic martyr who died fighting – and also therefore never grew up.

Michael Straight was completely devastated by the news, and this now played right into Anthony Blunt's hands in February 1937 – though, as with all spy recruitment stories, the exact details have been endlessly disputed, mulled over and besides. In essence Blunt asked Straight what he wanted to do on leaving Cambridge. The latter replied that he was contemplating becoming British – Whitney Straight had just done so – and work for the Labour Party. But Blunt had other ideas – he had 'friends' who wanted Straight to go back to the USA, to join Wall Street, and to work for the Communist International.

This caught Straight at a highly emotional and vulnerable moment, overwhelmed as he was by the thought of Cornford's revolutionary martyrdom in Spain. He felt pressured or trapped by Blunt's offer – though, as Penrose and Freeman point out, how he could have been so when it would have been so easy to say no is never explained and is therefore probably an attempt by Straight, narrating this years later, to put a good spin on what he was in effect now being asked to do – to betray his country in the interests of the USSR.

Straight was then introduced to a Russian agent – whom he disliked. But his sense of existential guilt and angst continued: 'My closest friend had given his life. I wanted to give mine'.

So when he went back to the USA in 1937 he was most certainly a Soviet source, if not actually a full-blown spy. And since, through his mother, he was part of one of the wealthiest and most influential families in the USA, he was able to get a job instantly at the heart of the US government, in the State Department (the US equivalent of the Foreign Office), for a while in the Department of the Interior, and as a speechwriter for the president, Franklin Roosevelt.

It is here that Straight's future career becomes vague in terms of espionage. In his memoirs *After Long Silence* he talks about various desultory meetings with a Soviet agent whom he identifies by the codename 'Michael Green'. One gets the impression from this that nothing of real value was handed over, but that Straight – who was now married, for the first time of three – was really going through the motions, out of loyalty to the memory of John Cornford and that of his Cambridge friends.

New evidence suggests that this is all nonsense. Research done in the Soviet archives suggests that Straight gave a much higher grade of secret away than those to which he admits in his memoirs and, as we can now see what he gave, it is clear that he, like Leo Long, completely downplayed his role as a spy.

However, it is obvious from the decrypts that, by 1942, Straight was no longer a spy for the NKVD, and he seems to have been the only one of the Cambridge spies to have been disgusted by the Nazi-Soviet Pact of 1939 (though presumably this did not stop him giving the USSR information for another three years). And, in 1942, he got a non-combatant military role, based well out of harm's way in the mid-west, in which he could serve in his country's armed forces without being in any danger of anyone trying to kill him.

Many sources name Straight as rather a dilettante and this seems to have been true of what would now become his journalistic and artistic career. He was lucky that his family owned a respected political journal *The New Republic* (which happily still exists under new ownership). This meant that he was able to swan around in media and artistic/literary circles without ever really having to work for a living – unlike his brother Whitney, back in Britain, whose hard-working career would culminate in being chairman of Rolls Royce.

It is obvious that while Straight had been a source for the NKVD, he was no longer one after the war. He does not appear directly in the later VENONA decrypt. However, his NKVD contacts do appear there (one codenamed BERG), as do numerous genuine American spies for the Soviet Union such as Alger Hiss or Harry Dexter White. (The latter committed suicide not long before; he would otherwise have been arrested for treason.)

The Australian writer Roland Perry does his best to claim that Straight was a spy for much longer but, while there is some very decent circumstantial evidence, the proof from the declassified archives does not provide any killer documentation that would nail down a case.

But there is no doubt about one thing. *Michael Straight knew who the key Cambridge spies were but did nothing about it, until 1963.* He tells the story in his memoirs of a trip to London for an Apostles reunion after the war in 1947, where he met both Blunt and Burgess. But he did nothing to inform anyone of the treachery of his friends, even though he was in a unique position so to do. By 1948 he claims (though with no evidence at all) that the British knew of his story.

And there is one bizarre story from 1948, told to his first wife, that a psychoanalyst had passed on in 1940 – a story that Burgess was a spy to someone in the British embassy in Washington. Historians believe that this is a true tale, but one that was unfortunately ignored by the British at the time. In 1951 Straight actually saw Burgess himself in Washington DC, but once again he did nothing – and, indeed, continued to do absolutely nothing until 1963.

Even then it was more good luck than anything else that finally persuaded Straight that he had to confess. He was offered the job of chairman of an advisory council on the arts, for which an FBI background check would be necessary. This ultimately proved the catalyst, and this time he confessed, naming Anthony Blunt as the person who had recruited him all those years go in Trinity College. He went to see an old friend, Arthur Schlesinger, a famous academic who was adding intellectual lustre to the Camelot aura of the Kennedy White House. Schlesinger contacted the Attorney General, Bobby Kennedy, and an interview was set up with the FBI.

It was probably not surprising, given Kim Philby's recent defection to the USSR, that the FBI took several months to bother to inform the British – by this time it was perhaps a question of who in MI5 and MI6 was actually on our side, so far as they were concerned. And that, in turn, might well explain the choice of British interrogator when one was eventually sent – Arthur Martin, who was soon to lose his job with MI5 as someone disruptive because, like the later infamous Peter Wright, he saw dozens of traitors where none existed.

With Straight's evidence, both Anthony Blunt and Leo Long were forced to confess past treason, though, as we saw, each was able to secure some kind of immunity deal and neither was prosecuted. Nor was Michael Straight. From 1969 to 1977 he was Deputy Chairman of the National Endowment for the Arts – Nixon is said not to have worried about Straight's past since he had by now, the president thought, changed sides.

And that in fact is the likely scenario – that Straight abandoned working for the NKVD in 1942, but failed to tell the authorities about Blunt and Burgess (and surely he must also have known of Philby, Maclean and Cairncross), and so waited until 1963, just weeks before Philby's defection to the USSR and Burgess' death earlier that year in Moscow.

So, as some have written, Straight himself might have sent no one to their deaths. Indeed, he was probably as dilettante a spy as he was everything else; a rich kid who would never have been taken seriously as a journalist, or as the novelist he now became, but for his enormous list of hereditary connections and the ability to coast through life without the need to earn a living.

But his silence was very costly – all those who did die as a result of the Cambridge spies' treachery can be laid to him as well since, if they had been discovered much sooner, those whom they betrayed to the NKVD would never have died.

He continued to move in exalted circles though. His second wife was Nina Auchincloss, Gore Vidal's half-sister and thus stepsister to Jackie Kennedy (whom he knew socially).

Straight's secret lasted a long time, until Blunt was unveiled in 1979. Then his exposure was swift, and it is interesting that, although his guilt as being part of the spy ring was evident, no one took him seriously as a Fifth Man or Sixth Man – until after his death when Roland Perry's *The Last of the Cold War Spies* suggested a perhaps greater role than others. Straight's unreadable *After Long Silence* in

1983 did not really convince anyone and, although he wanted always to be remembered for his literary output, when he died in January 2004 it was as a spy and not as a novelist.

But were there other spies? To this great molehunt we must now turn...

WHO ELSE AND OTHER POSSIBILITIES: A Conclusion

So we now know that the Fifth Man was none other than John Cairncross. But we also know that Michael Straight was a Cambridge spy and so too were Leo Long and Alan Nunn May. To me that makes at least eight, and so there were eight men who spied for Russia who went to Cambridge during the 1930s.

This, therefore, makes somewhat silly a book title such as one that appeared called *The Fifth Man.* There is no doubting the total sincerity of its author, who really did believe that his candidate was indeed one of the Cambridge spy ring, and was number 5 on the list. But there were at least eight, not merely five, and so to add to the list that I have just outlined would make any book on yet more Cambridge spies need to be entitled *At Least The Ninth Man* or something to that effect!

And were there nine or ten men? Or women? This is a rather all-male book but, as we now also know, not a few women served as immensely brave agents behind enemy lines for Britain during the Second World War, most notably for SOE, such as Vera Atkins and 'Garbo', to name just two of them. And, once spies could emerge from the shadows, we discover that Daphne Park (later Baroness Park of Monmouth) was a spy for MI6, and that the Security Service, MI5, had two women chiefs, Dame Stella Rimington and Eliza (later Baroness) Manningham-Buller; both of them quasi-role models for the wonderful portrayal by Judi Dench as M in the James Bond films.

However, the official history of MI5 names no new names. This has not prevented plenty of people from guessing. As the earlier chapters hinted, all sorts of entirely innocent people have been accused of being traitors upon what one can best describe as circumstantial evidence. And then there were the slightly paranoid leaks to the press of Peter Wright, the rogue MI5 operative who later went public through his autobiography *Spycatcher*.

Why do we think that there were more spies than the ones about which we know already? Maybe there were far more than the ones who were exposed, but it is equally possible that we have, in fact, discovered all of them. Either interpretation is, of course, equally plausible!

I think it comes back to conspiracy theories, and the way that we love them. Surely, we say, Lee Harvey Oswald *must* have had accomplices to kill Kennedy. Diana could not have died so tragically for the banal reason that she was not wearing a seatbelt that fateful night... And sometimes conspiracy theories get nasty, such as the widespread belief in many parts of the world in the nineteenth century Russian forgery, *The Protocols of Zion,* that posits a global

Jewish threat to dominate the world. This was believed by Nazis in the twentieth century and, alas, today by many in Arab-speaking countries (as a quick search on YouTube of news programmes will swiftly and sadly confirm).

So it is with spies. The old KGB, now in several forms as the FSB and SVR, naturally still wish us to believe in their omnipotence and that they really did have Reds under many beds and that their tentacles spread everywhere. Yet, as I hope we have shown, the KGB was nothing like as successful all the time as it wanted people in the west to think, and that many of their successes were entirely good luck rather than part of an all-pervasive master plan.

And we also know from the success of Oleg Gordievsky that the traffic went both ways, with leading members of the KGB coming over to our side. It is interesting that MI6 always offers lifelong anonymity to agents who want it when they cross over to the west, and so there may equally be many totally obscure Soviet defectors whose loyalty to Britain or the USA will forever be secret. Most of us want as many people as possible to be aware of our successes, but MI6 is one of the very few organisations for whom their greatest achievements must always remain secret and in the shadows.

Two thoughts remain, before we can look at a couple of Cambridge graduates who have each been suspected of being spies for the Soviets, but who were almost certainly nothing of the kind. Let us look at the argument on both sides of the debate on whether or not more spies existed than we have been told.

The Russians have always loved to trumpet their successes. To me it seems rather far-fetched to think that there is some major spy out there somewhere who worked for years for the KGB without his former employers (many of whom now rule Russia, such as ex-KGB officer Vladimir Putin) wanting to brag about it in one form or another. They love writing about the Magnificent Five to show, in their view, how they bested the British establishment at its supposed heart in Cambridge, and if there really had been a significant Tenth or Eleventh Man, I feel certain that *the Russians* would have told us by now. But they have not – and maybe because there were none.

On the other hand, it always seems strange, for example, that there were no Oxford spies to match those recruited at Cambridge. (Your author has degrees from both Oxford and Cambridge universities so, like many of the people described in this book, could be said therefore to have dual loyalties, especially on Boat Race day!) Only one relatively obscure Oxford graduate, Arthur Wynn, a minor civil servant and called Agent Scott has been named as a Soviet spy (and even he had links to Cambridge University – maybe he is therefore our Ninth Man!).

Yet it seems strange that, however superior Cambridge graduates feel themselves to those of Oxford, that the NKVD would agree with this assessment and recruit only from the slightly younger of England's two ancient universities. Were Oxford people more patriotic? Did they believe that you could be a genuine Marxist without spying for Russia? Or did they simply grow up and realise that the USSR under Stalin was an illusion and, especially after August 1939, no different from the monstrous Nazi dictatorship that they all so rightly feared and loathed back in the 1930s.

However, no Oxford spy has emerged, and certainly not on the scale of those from Cambridge. It does seem somewhat odd, but for want of better information and a look at MI5 files that have not been cleared to appear in the official history, we shall never find out.

(Cambridge graduates would, of course, reject the notion that Oxford graduates, being cleverer than their Light Blue counterparts by the Cam, were *so clever* that they were Soviet spies and never got caught... Perish the very thought of it!)

People have nevertheless made some stabs at working out who any as yet unmasked Soviet spies from the 1930s might have been.

Alister Watson (1908–1981) was an Apostle, and a fellow of King's College Cambridge, and was for certain a member of the Communist party while there, and a contemporary at university of Anthony Blunt. He is thought of mainly for his scientific achievements and intellectual pursuits – he knew the philosopher Ludwig Wittgenstein, for instance – but he has also been rumoured, without firm evidence, to have been an NKVD spy.

Also sometimes suggested is Sir Dennis Proctor (1905–1983), who would have been slightly older than the main group of Cambridge recruits. At King's he joined the Apostles, and became firmly convinced of Marxist analysis. He always professed to be 'left wing', while insisting, through his many decades working for the Treasury and later as Permanent Secretary to the Ministry of Power, that, as a civil servant, he should never let his views get in the way of giving impartial advice to his political masters.

With the Apostles he became, to his later detriment, a good friend both of Blunt and Burgess – he got married in 1936 so shared their politics and their aesthetic interests but not other facets of their lives. He was Chairman of the Tate Gallery in the 1950s and his love of the arts gave him lifelong links to Blunt at the Courtauld, of which he was one of the Governors.

So, when Blunt confessed in 1964, Proctor was eventually interrogated by MI5 two years later. (Why the gap, one wonders?) It emerged that he was one of Burgess' best sources, which put Proctor under much suspicion though, as he told his interrogators, while he had told many things to Burgess, he had 'no real secrets to give'.

Was he a spy? In the end MI5 thought not, and no case was pursued. Does this make him innocent or guilty? How can we know? And here I feel sure that, if he had indeed been an NKVD and later KGB agent, somehow, in view of the importance and strategic nature of his later career, someone in the KGB would have crowed with glee somewhere and that, as a result, we would know for sure. Yet that has not happened in his case, and so I feel that we must do what juries are requested in this country and presume innocence until guilt is proved.

(But if he was guilty his access to top secrets would put that of known spy John Cairncross into the shade...)

Two other people have been extensively investigated as possible spies. One is very much in public. The other was a household name until his death, only in very recent years, and is now suspected by some because of the opening to the public on the file on him held by MI5 and the forthcoming book on this issue by his equally well-known daughter.

The first of these is Victor Rothschild, 3rd Lord Rothschild (1910–1990), a graduate of Trinity College (like Burgess, Blunt, Cairncross and Philby) and, like Blunt and Burgess and the last two people we saw, Proctor and Watson, a member of the notorious Apostles.

Rothschild was essentially a scientist, despite his famous family background and his inheritance of the Rothschild title in 1937. His expertise, for which he won two Cambridge doctorates, was initially on the fertilisation of the eggs of frogs – not, one would think, an issue of massive importance to the intelligence service of any country!

But, as the writer Kenneth Rose puts it, in his biography of Rothschild for the *Dictionary of National Biography*:

'The carefree friendships of Rothschild's early Cambridge years that had continued throughout the war cast a shadow over the last decade of his life. The defection of Burgess to Russia and the uncovering of Blunt as a Soviet agent exposed Rothschild to innuendo and vilification in press and parliament.'

If anything this is an understatement. In particular, after 1979 and Blunt's very public exposure, Rothschild, who owned the house in which Burgess and Blunt had lived during the war, was bombarded with requests to know whether or not he too had been a traitor. (And remember that one of Burgess' covers during the 1930s was giving supposed investment advice to Rothschild's mother.)

Rothschild had been in MI5 during the Second World War, but not anything of remote interest to the NKVD, since his speciality was counter-sabotage, something for which he was ideally trained as a scientist. He was awarded the George Medal, the second highest decoration for civilian bravery after the George Cross, for his work in bomb disposal. But perhaps his most famous achievement, unearthed by Churchill's archivist Allen Packwood, was his analysis of some cigars sent to Churchill, to find out whether or not they were explosive. (Thankfully for all of us they were not.)

He then spent years in a mix of agricultural research and work for Royal Dutch Shell, co-ordinating that oil giant's whole research and development programme until he joined the Civil Service as the first Head of what was then called the Central Policy Review Staff.

It is unlikely that an agricultural researcher would have mattered to the Soviets, and when he was made head of the CPRS in 1971 his past would have been gone through with a fine-toothed comb because, by this time, everyone knew about the treachery of his friends Blunt and Burgess. Since this body reported directly to the Cabinet and the Prime Minister, its members would have been vetted to the highest degree. And, like its less distinguished staffers, the chairman was equally investigated – and passed.

Until 1979 he was safe. But then the storm came of Blunt's outing as a spy and the world descended on Rothschild. He knew he was innocent and, what is more, he had been cleared by the most paranoid of molehunters, the spycatcher himself, Peter Wright. But, as Rothschild's various biographers have been correct to say, Wright was a poisoned chalice, a man with a deep grievance against his former employers at MI5 and with a powerful agenda of his own. So, while Wright's testimony was accurate, Rothschild became enveloped in the former's own machinations and wild conspiracy theories, not remotely to the latter's advantage. At one stage Rothschild even went to the lengths of writing to the press to declare his own innocence!

Those who know him say that this cost him his health and eventually his life, and he died on 20 March 1990. His second wife, Tess, who died in 1996, had also been in MI5 during the war, and like him knew many in the politically liberal circle around the Apostles.

Death did not preserve him or his wife, however, since dead people cannot sue. Books appeared casting strong suspicion on him, naming him, as we saw, as the Fifth Man, and certainly as a spy of some kind or another. Yet if even Wright, who saw spies everywhere, was convinced of his innocence, not to mention those who vetted him in the 1970s (and again after Blunt's exposure) were as well, who are we not to? I feel sure that in his case, while he might have been retrospectively very unwise in his choice of friends – or better, simply unlucky – he was the patriot that he always professed to be.

The other person purported to be a spy certainly surprised me – Jacob Bronowski, whose magnificent 1973 television series *The Ascent of Man* showed to millions that science could make viewing every much as gripping as the arts, and which has paved the way for the many successful scientific documentaries ever since.

Here I should say that study of Bronowski's possible links with intelligence is very much at an early stage, and that his daughter, the equally distinguished writer and historian Lisa Jardine, will tell us the details at some future date, when her book is published. (What follows is partly from a lecture that she gave in public at the University of Hull, with which, in an earlier form, her father was closely associated early in his career.)

Bronowski (1908–1974) was born to a Jewish family in what is now Poland but, thankfully for him, came to Britain in 1920, thereby avoiding all the horrors that befell those who stayed behind. A brilliant mathematician from an early age, he gained a First from Jesus College, Cambridge, and then became a wrangler, meaning that he was one of the top mathematicians of his time.

In 1934 he went to what was then called University College Hull, where he stayed for the next eight years. Note the timing – he had left Cambridge by the time that the main spies were being recruited through 'Otto', and that he was not at Trinity, King's or Trinity Hall.

By 1942 he was being considered for war work, and this is where, it seems, life became interesting! He believed deeply in what we now call continuing education: bringing learning to people well outside normal university circles. And here he got into trouble – not that he would have known this at that time or, indeed, possibly at any stage in his life, as it is only now that the close surveillance under which the police and MI5 put him has emerged from the secrecy of the files. In short, his left-wing views caused him to be regarded very askance by the vetting authorities so, when he was allowed to do war work in 1942, his clearance was limited by establishment doubts concerning his loyalties.

In 1945 he was the scientific deputy to the official delegation of the British Joint Chiefs of Staff Mission to examine the effects of the atomic bombs dropped on Japan, upon which he wrote a highly influential and important report. While his security classification was restricted in Britain, this appears not to have been the case in his pre-trip visit to the USA, where he met everyone of significance in the development of the atomic bomb.

After this his life became rather more prosaic, working as a scientist for the National Coal Board – surely again something not likely to have been of massive interest to the KGB. But he also became well-known as a broadcaster and consultant on scientific issues to the BBC, and by 1971 this latter link was to transform his life and the way in which science is portrayed on television. That year he was asked to make the scientific equivalent of the 1969 series by Kenneth Clark called *Civilization*, the first intellectual blockbuster of its kind and, after two years of filming, *The Ascent of Man* came out to vast acclaim in 1973.

By this time he had emigrated to California, to work (near Francis Crick, the co-discoverer of DNA) at the Salk Institute of Biological Sciences in San Diego, founded by Jonas Salk, whose own research led to the creation of mass-produced polio vaccine.

Sadly he did not have much time to enjoy his deserved fame since he died the following year in 1974.

And there things have rested until MI5's file on him became public and his daughter's first Jacob Bronowski lecture at Hull University in October 2012, when she revealed to the audience how her father had been seen as a security risk by MI5 during the war.

So was he a spy? Again, as with Lord Rothschild, I think not. Plenty of people had 'progressive' views in the 1930s and plenty of them had fond illusions about the USSR that were soon shattered when the true nature of Stalin's Russia became all too apparent. Being left wing, even being a life-long socialist, does not make one into a spy, since there is a huge gap between holding to an ideological belief and actually betraying one's country. As a Pole, Bronowski is unlikely to have been sanguine when the USSR and Third Reich partitioned his homeland in 1939 to 1940.

And there is therefore an irony here. The non-spy, Bronowski, was given only limited security access by the British during the war, whereas the actual atomic bomb spies, Alan Nunn May and, above all, Klaus Fuchs, saw everything, and really were working for the NKVD. MI5 was looking – and in the wrong place.

Were there others? By now most of them would either be dead or very elderly and immensely frail, so it is unlikely that we will ever know. But the story of the Cambridge spies we *do* know about is surely exciting enough.

END

Acknowledgements

All too often acknowledgements end with a thank you to the patient wife of the author so let me start this with acknowledging my wife Paulette. She is my companion, muse, inspiration and best friend, and without her none of my books would ever get written.

Today far too many publishers are part of large conglomerates – the days of the gentleman publisher are rapidly becoming extinct. (One of my former publishers is now owned by a French family that also has missile defence interests, which gives you some idea...) Thankfully that is not the case with Oleander Press and its owner Jon Gifford. And, in a day in which the publisher's lunch has long since departed, he has resurrected the publisher's coffee, which has kept both me and other Oleander authors awake and able to write.

This book was inspired by such a conversation over coffee, and here profound thanks go to the well-known Heffers bookseller Richard Reynolds, friend and encourager of various Cambridge authors, and whose enthusiasm and knowledge is recognised in his chairmanship of the Gold Dagger Award Panel of the Crime Writers' Association. He and his wife Sally are a source of much support and kindness to me and my wife.

And it is Sally's niece Sarah Mehta whom I am happy to thank as the editor for this book – as always, all mistakes that might have crept through are my errors and not hers.

In the Preface I gave warmest professional thanks to Professor Christopher Andrew, without whom the historical study of intelligence would never have happened, or certainly not on the scale which has now occurred. Once again interpretations in this book are mine, but his pioneering work is invaluable to all who work in this field – my first formal academic intelligence history work, on SOE and OSS in the former Yugoslavia in World War II, is well under way thanks to Christopher and to his main assistant Dr Peter Martland, to whom I am also most grateful.

I am an attendee at their Intelligence History seminar at Corpus College (where we meet near a portrait of Christopher Marlowe, the Elizabethan spy). The rules are quite simple – either you cannot say *who* said something there, or you cannot say what *X* said. Otherwise such a seminar would by definition be impossible. So anything I have learned over the years has to be described as deep background, and since this book, not being academic, does not need footnotes, I can write without direct attribution, but with much gratitude to many a fascinating speaker over the years, and from more than one country.

The University Library in Cambridge is a copyright library so has millions of books, many of which were vital to my research for this book, and I am most grateful to the staff of the CUL (including the tea room) for making it such a congenial place in which to work.

For some of the time writing this work I have been subsidised by a fascinating Brazilian 'study abroad' programme based in Cambridge, with numerous students from Porto Alegre, Goiania, Sao Paolo, Bauru, Fortaleza and Rio (including a girl who really is from Ipanema). But I am especially grateful to Professor Geoffrey Williams and his wife Janice, who run the Cambridge INSTEP Program that brings many exceptionally bright American students to Cambridge for a Semester Abroad of study, usually in their junior year. I have been teaching the Cold War for many very happy years now and it is an exceptionally pleasant way of earning a living.

And I am grateful to Churchill College, Cambridge, where I am a current Associate, and an Emeritus Archives By-Fellow, whose Winston Churchill Archives collection must be the nicest place to work in Cambridge. I am also a happy Visitor to St Edmund's College, Cambridge and, during the writing of this book I have had the pleasure of supervising excellent undergraduates from Robinson and Homerton Colleges about British history since 1867. Once more, a splendid way to earn a living.

I am most grateful to Eileen Gunn and to the Trustees of the Royal Literary Fund, for their wonderful and life-saving three-year grant. This has enabled me to concentrate upon writing, and this is the first of the books that could not have been written without their generous support.

Last but by no means least, thank you very much to family and to friends, including the wonderful staff at

Heffers, Cambridge's rightly famous bookshop, and to my parents Frederick and Elizabeth Catherwood who have retired to not far from where I am writing this. As ever special thanks go to Andrew and Clare Whittaker (and their children Charlotte and Rosie) and to Alasdair and Rachel Paine and Nathan and Debbie Buttery, and their respective descendants.

Christopher Catherwood
Cambridge, January 2013

Printed in Great Britain
by Amazon

70341919R00129